A Warden's Path

From Tough to Smart on Crime

By Percy Pitzer

Edited by
Jason Roberson

THREEFOLD
PUBLISHING

Contents

Introduction – Retirement Reflection

I retired in 1998. After 25 years of service, starting as a correctional officer and eventually serving as a prison warden at three separate prisons, it was time to step away. My retirement was made possible by a shift in federal policy—President Bill Clinton transitioned us from the Civil Service Retirement System to the Federal Employees Retirement System, which allowed me to retire two years earlier than I had initially planned.

I spent my final years at the United States Penitentiary in Beaumont, Texas. This facility, part of the Beaumont Federal Correctional Complex, opened in 1996 to house some of the country's most dangerous criminals. It was built to relieve the overcrowding in other high-security facilities, a problem that had plagued the federal system for years. Beaumont, perhaps unfairly, had a reputation that stuck due to the perceived violence within its walls. Every day, I walked that compound, witnessing the harsh reality of incarceration. I saw men turn into shells of themselves, weighed down by the gravity of their pasts and the bleakness of their futures.

Part of the Beaumont Federal Correctional Complex

As I prepared to leave that life behind, I couldn't help but reflect on the men I saw pass through my gates—some deserving of their fate, others who, I believed, had served longer sentences than necessary. My heart ached for the men who would soon be released, knowing full well the hardships they would endure. Society does not welcome ex-felons with open arms. Landlords refuse to rent to them, and employers are hesitant to hire them. The cycle is vicious, and the statistics are sobering—nearly 68% of released prisoners are rearrested within three years, and over 75% within five years. The reasons are many: lack of employment opportunities, the stigma of a criminal record, and the inability to reintegrate into a world that has moved on without them. Many would find their way back into the system simply because they know no other way to survive.

One inmate came to mind: Darius Kendell Braxton. He was just 18 years old when he was sentenced, still barely more than a kid himself. Four years earlier, in a reckless and desperate moment, he made the fateful decision to carjack someone on the north side of Beaumont. But it wasn't just a carjacking—inside the vehicle was a passenger, turning his crime into a federal kidnapping offense. Had it happened a few years earlier, he might have faced state charges with a lighter sentence. But in 1992, Congress passed the Carjacking Statute, and in 1994, the Violent Crime Control and Law Enforcement Act strengthened it, leaving no room for leniency. The law was clear, and so was his fate: mandatory sentencing guidelines ensured he would spend years behind bars. Wrong crime, wrong time.

When Darius first arrived at USP Beaumont, he carried himself with the defiance of someone too young to grasp the full weight of his situation. He got into fights with other inmates, clashed with correctional officers—every decision he made seemed to push him further down a dangerous path. I often wondered how someone like him could survive in a place like this. Beaumont was no place for an 18-year-old, no place for someone who still had a chance to change. Inmates like him had only two choices: become prey or become predators—there was no middle ground. Every day was a test of survival. Who could he trust? Who would turn on him?

I watched him and thought about the future that awaited him beyond these walls. Would he grow into a man hardened by his environment, unable to imagine life beyond the prison gates? Or would he learn to navigate the unwritten rules of survival, only to walk free into a world that had no place for him? Even if he made it out alive, what then? A parole officer watching his every step, potential employers slamming doors in his face, old friends tempting him back into the life that put him here in the first place. His crime was serious—no one could deny that. But so was the question that haunted me: What ~~pens when we send a kid to a place designed to turn men into~~ ~~orse?~~

~~orking in this system, and I owe it everything. I~~ ~~a step behind, struggling to get ahead.~~ ~~e, the favor of the good Lord, I~~ ~~mily. This job gave me secu-~~ ~~lked away, I felt the weight of~~ ~~sustained me. I wanted to give~~ ~~going wrong, but I didn't quite~~

~~hed for a way to make a difference.~~

Because while I may have left the prison, the prison would never leave me. I had seen men enter these walls hardened by the world, some beyond saving, others desperate for a second chance.

I often asked myself—how did I get here? How did a boy from a quiet town, a boy who once believed the world was fair and simple, end up leading a place like this?

To answer that, I must take you back. Back before I understood the weight of justice, before I saw the cracks in the system, before I ever imagined I'd wear a warden's badge.

Part One

LEARNING

Chapter 1

Humble Beginnings

I was just seven years old when my father passed away, leaving my mother to raise my two brothers and me on her own. That kind of loss stays with a person, but at that age, I didn't fully grasp the weight of it. What I did understand was that something essential was missing in our home—and that my mother was doing everything in her power to fill that void, not just emotionally, but financially too.

We lived in a modest log house nestled between Boscobel and Blue River, Wisconsin. Back then, in the 1950s, it was a quiet stretch of land— rural, rugged, and for the most part, safe. There were no flashing sirens in the night, no fear of walking home from school. The crime rate in Boscobel was practically nonexistent. Compared to a city like Beaumont, Texas in 2025, where the violent crime rate now hovers around 12 per

I grew up in this modest log cabin nestled between Boscobel and Blue River, Wisconsin—a quiet, rural stretch of land back in the 1950s.

3

1,000 residents—well over four times the national average—Boscobel back then felt like another planet. We didn't lock our doors. Trouble, if it existed, didn't come from strangers with guns or gangs on street corners. It came in quieter forms: broken appliances, unpaid bills, and empty cupboards.

We were poor, though as a kid, I didn't know to call it that. It was just life. We didn't dwell on what we didn't have. We made do, often with things that were secondhand or patched together. I thought everyone's shoes had worn soles and mismatched laces. I thought every mother worked three jobs and still came home to cook dinner.

My mother was the hardest-working person I've ever known. She relied on welfare to help make ends meet—not because she wanted to, but because she had to. But even with that, she never sat idle. She took in ironing, long hours spent pressing shirts and dresses with a focus and care that, looking back, was almost surgical. On weekends, she cooked at a supper club, coming home long after we'd gone to bed, the scent of fried food and fatigue clinging to her clothes. In the summer months, she worked at a canning factory. Her hands were often red and raw from the hours spent sorting and sealing produce, but she never complained-not once. No job was beneath her if it meant putting food on our table.

Then there was that one afternoon when I was twelve. I came home from school and found her sitting at the kitchen table, crying. It was a sight I'd never seen before, and it stopped me cold. My mother didn't cry—at least not in front of us. I asked her what was wrong, and she told me her iron had broken. Just an iron. But for her, that iron wasn't just an appliance—it was her livelihood. Without it, she couldn't finish the day's work, and without that work, there'd be no paycheck that week.

I didn't say anything. I just turned around and walked down to the hardware store. I had a paper route, made maybe three or four bucks a week, just enough for a soda and a pack of gum. But I asked the owner if I could charge an iron and pay him back a dollar a week.

I still remember the look on his face—he was surprised, maybe even a little amused. But then he nodded and said yes.

I carried that iron home as if it were made of gold. When I set it in front of my mother, she cried again—but those were different tears. Tears of relief, of gratitude. When I told her how I got it, she pulled me in and held me tight. That moment seared itself into my memory. That was the first time I understood what responsibility really looked like. Not the kind people talk about in speeches or slogans, but the kind that requires sacrifice and action.

Years later, when I became a warden, I found myself drawing on those memories more often than I ever expected. Many of the men I oversaw grew up in poverty, just like I did—except their poverty came with different risks. In Boscobel, our biggest fear was falling behind on the light bill. For many of these men, growing up poor meant dodging violence, joining gangs for protection, and making impossible choices at a young age.

I could relate to their hunger, their frustration, their sense that no one was coming to help. And while I never excused criminal behavior, I did understand the road that led many of them to prison wasn't all that different from the road I traveled. The difference often came down to timing, influence, or one small opportunity that someone else didn't get.

The correctional system back in the 1950s looked nothing like what it is today. Back then, incarceration was often about containment and discipline—there was little talk of rehabilitation or mental health. Today, we face far more complex challenges: mass incarceration, racial disparities, mental illness, addiction. We have prisons that are overcrowded, understaffed, and increasingly violent.

But one thing hasn't changed: the people inside still carry the burdens of where they came from. Many of them were born into situations that made prison feel like a foregone conclusion. And when I think about my own upbringing—the worn-out shoes, the broken iron, the silent resilience of my mother—I'm reminded that poverty doesn't just make you go without; it shapes how you see the world.

It gave me empathy. It gave me grit. And it taught me that leadership—real leadership—starts with remembering where you came from.

School, on the other hand, was a different kind of challenge. I managed to get through most of it, but I wouldn't call myself a dedicated student. High school wasn't my favorite chapter. I made it halfway through my junior year at Boscobel High, but I was more interested in hanging out with my friends than focusing on textbooks. One afternoon, I was at Dutch's pool hall—a local hangout where we spent time after school—when the Chief of Police walked in. He didn't say much, just looked at me and asked me to come with him. His tone was calm, but something about it made my stomach tighten.

The walk to the station was silent. I kept glancing over at him, searching his face for some kind of clue, but he gave nothing away. When we arrived, I stepped inside and immediately noticed a U.S. Army Staff Sergeant seated in the office. My heart pounded against my ribs. I still didn't know exactly why I was there, but I could feel it —something was wrong.

The Sergeant wasted no time. He looked me in the eye and delivered the news: my brother, Richard (Dick) Pitzer, was missing in action in Vietnam. The words didn't register at first. Missing. It didn't mean he was dead, not yet. It meant they didn't know where he was. It meant maybe—just maybe—he could still come home.

Then the Sergeant asked me to do something I wasn't prepared for. He needed me to accompany him to deliver the news to my mother.

Even now, all these years later, the memory of that day in March of 1968 still brings tears to my eyes. It was the hardest moment of my life. I sat in the car with the Sergeant, staring out the window, trying to find the right words, but nothing came. What was I supposed to say? How was I supposed to look my mother in the eyes and tell her that the son she had fought so hard to raise was missing in a war halfway across the world?

When we walked through the door, she knew. She could see it on my face. I don't remember exactly what I said—just that it shattered her. We held on to hope for seven long days, waiting for news, praying for a miracle. Every time the phone rang, my stomach clenched. Every time someone knocked on the door, my heart pounded.

Then, the final notification arrived—his body had been recovered.

This is my older brother, CPL Richard (Dick) Pitzer who was killed in action in Vietnam on March 6, 1968.

Dick was gone. Just like that, the hope we had been clinging to was gone. My mother, who had already endured so much, had to bury her son. And I had to learn another painful lesson: focus on today, because tomorrow isn't promised.

SGT Terry Gilbertson, *Boscobel, Wisconsin was killed in action in Vietnam on February 28, 1968.* **CPL Richard (Dick) Pitzer**, *Boscobel, Wisconsin was killed in action in Vietnam on March 6, 1968.* **PFC Leland Radley**, *Boscobel, Wisconsin was killed in action in Vietnam on August 25, 1968. Imagine a small town with a population of just 2,608, where two young men died in Vietnam within a single week, and a third was killed four months later.*

That moment changed me forever. It stripped away any illusions I had about the world being fair. It forced me to grow up in ways I hadn't expected. I understood what it meant to carry the weight of responsibility, to face difficult truths head-on.

And in many ways, it set me on the path that eventually led me to a career in corrections. When you've lived through hardship, when you've stood at the edge of grief and seen what loss can do to a family, you develop a certain resolve. You learn to see people for who they are, not just for their mistakes. You understand that everyone carries their own burdens, their own stories of struggle and survival.

Life didn't take it easy on me, but in the end, it made me who I am. And for that, I am grateful.

At 17, filled with disappointment, sadness, and anger, I dropped out of high school and joined the Army. I felt like I had nowhere else to turn, and the military seemed like the only viable path forward. On

May 20, 1968, I boarded a bus and headed for Fort Campbell, Kentucky, for basic training. The ride there was long and quiet, filled with self-doubt and thoughts of the unknown. The Army became my escape, my way of proving something to myself and the world. I was eager to prove I could be strong, that I could stand on my own, but I had no idea what was waiting for me.

Percy Pitzer, age 17

Upon completing basic training, I was assigned to Fort Dix, New Jersey, for advanced infantry training. My heart was set on Vietnam; I wanted to be in the fight, to make a difference, to take control of a world that felt out of my hands. I thought the war would give me purpose, that it would answer the questions I didn't even know how to ask. However, because of my age, I was sent to a unit in Germany instead. It felt like an insult, like I was being sidelined from the real action. I spent my days training, feeling the weight of my growing restlessness. The moment I turned eighteen, I volunteered for Vietnam and received the requested transfer. I had no idea what I was truly signing up for. My mind was set, but my heart had not yet been tested.

I will never forget my sergeant pleading with me not to transfer to Vietnam. He was a seasoned soldier, a man who had seen more than his share of war, and he knew the horrors that awaited. He saw something I couldn't at the time. He knew what it meant to lose friends, to see the worst parts of humanity up close. But I was young, foolish, and full of anger—I refused to listen. I was determined, stubborn, and, in retrospect, utterly blind to the bigger picture. Looking back, I realize how selfish that decision was. What I never considered was the pressure I was putting on my mother, who had already lost one son in the war. I guess you might say it was more of a revenge decision than a commonsense decision. A rational mind would have never put my mother in the position of potentially losing another son. I only thought about proving something to myself, to the world, to the memory of my lost brother.

After serving between four and five months in the jungles of Vietnam, we received a rare visit from the Commanding General of the 4th Infantry Division. It was an unusual sight, a high-ranking officer standing in the thick of the same mud and misery we trudged through every day. He came to the field and spoke with each of us. His presence was both reassuring and surreal. He asked how we were doing, and we all responded with the expected "fine" and moved on with our duties. We had grown accustomed to masking the truth. What I didn't know was that following his visit, he sent letters to each of our families, reassuring our family members that he had spoken with us and that we were "safe and in good spirits." My mother wrote back.

When I read her letter in Vietnam, I could feel every ounce of her fear and love spilling through the ink. She had written back to the man who'd checked on me, thanking him with raw emotion. She told him she had already lost one son in Vietnam and couldn't bear the thought of losing another. I remember sitting there, holding that letter, and wondering what must have been going through her mind as she wrote those words. Did she cry, the way I did when I read them? Did she stop and pray that someone—anyone—might have the heart to intervene? That letter did more than just reach me. It reached someone who had the power to act. And it reminded me that I mattered.

That experience—of being seen, remembered, and loved—stays with me. And it's given me a deeper understanding of what letters mean to people who are cut off from the world. I think about inmates, locked away and often forgotten, who receive letters from their mothers. The emotional power of those messages must be enormous. Because I know what it meant to me.

A letter like that tells you you're still someone's child. You're still loved. You're still worth the effort. For someone behind bars, those words might be the only reminder of who they were before the system gave them a number. That kind of connection isn't just comforting—it's life-giving.

Psychologists have found that inmates who get regular mail from loved ones show lower levels of depression and anxiety. That doesn't surprise me. I remember the anticipation of holding an envelope with my name on it. That simple act broke through the isolation. And studies show that those connections matter—emotionally and behaviorally. Inmates who stay in touch with their families are more likely to behave well, to participate in programs, and to succeed when they're finally released. Some studies even show lower recidivism rates just from maintaining that bond.

But beyond the data, I think of the human truth I lived: that a letter can hold someone together. My mother poured her grief, her hope, her desperate love into that letter—and it found its way to me. To this day, I can still feel her presence in every word.

So, when I think about a mother writing to her son in prison, I don't see a letter—I see a lifeline. A prayer in paper form. And I know, from experience, just how powerful that can be.

Approximately one month after that visit, still deep in the jungle, a radio message came into my unit. We were ordered to cut a landing zone immediately because a chopper was coming in to pick up Pitzer. My heart dropped. My first thought was that something had happened to my mother. I braced for the worst. The feeling of dread was overwhelming, unlike anything I had experienced before. My body felt frozen, my mind raced through possibilities. When I returned to the base, an escort was waiting to take me to a Major.

The Major sat me down, looked me in the eyes, and asked if I had a brother killed in Vietnam. I confirmed. His next words changed everything. I would be leaving the country the next day for Thailand. It was not a request; it was an order. My mother's letter had made its way through the chain of command, and someone had decided that she would not lose another son to war. It was an act of compassion, a rare glimmer of mercy in a brutal world. I should have felt relieved, but guilt immediately settled in. Why me? Why was I given an escape when so many others weren't? I thought about my fellow soldiers, the bonds we had formed, the trust we had built. How could I leave them behind?

A New Beginning: Lessons in Leadership, Love, and Resilience in Thailand

When I arrived in Bangkok, my first action was to call my mother. The moment I heard her voice, I knew she had been waiting by the phone, dreading the worst, praying for the best. Her voice trembled with concern, not for herself, but for me. She was afraid I would be angry with her for writing the letter. The last thing she wanted was to upset me. Instead, I reassured her. I told her all was good and that the decision I made to go to Vietnam was the reckless choice of an immature kid. I expressed deep regret that I had ever put her in that position. We both cried, sharing a moment of deep understanding, and we never spoke of it again.

This sudden turn of events left me with a storm of emotions. I was relieved but also burdened. I had left my fellow soldiers behind in the jungle, knowing they would continue the fight without me. The guilt weighed heavily, but so did the realization that someone had shown me mercy. A thoughtful superior, moved by my mother's words, had changed the course of my life. I was given a second chance.

Memories of my brother, the relentless humidity of the jungle, the camaraderie of my unit, and every letter from home became the foundation on which I built my future. Each experience, every hardship, every moment of fear and hope, etched indelible marks on my soul. They shaped me into the man I would become, a man who would forever carry the lessons of war, love, and sacrifice. They reminded me that life is fragile, that the bonds we form in times of hardship never truly fade. And, most importantly, they taught me that love—especially a mother's love—has the power to change fate itself.

Thailand was a whirlwind of new experiences and lessons, shaping me in ways I never could have imagined. After a few days in Bangkok, I was transferred to Korat, a place that, until that moment, had been nothing more than a name on a map. Unlike many of my fellow servicemen, I wasn't assigned to an infantry unit—there weren't any stationed in Thailand. Instead, I was given the daunting role of military police advisor for a Thai security unit. At just eighteen years old, the weight of that responsibility was staggering. I could barely take care of myself, and yet, here I was, expected to advise seasoned men, many of whom had been serving far longer than I had even been alive. The pressure was immense, and I often questioned whether I was truly up to the task.

It didn't take long to realize that leadership wasn't about barking orders—it was about listening, understanding, and earning respect. In those early days, I felt the weight of my inexperience pressing down on me, but I quickly learned three key lessons that would shape the rest of my life. First, to be successful with a group, one must listen more than speak. It wasn't about proving how much I knew, but rather about understanding the strengths and weaknesses of the men around me. Second, leadership isn't something you're born with; it's a skill that can be developed with patience, practice, and humility. And third, real power isn't wielded with an iron fist—it's shared, delegated, and cultivated through trust and teamwork. With this philosophy, and by the grace of God, I found my footing in my new role, gradually growing into the leader I had been tasked to be.

Despite the challenges of my assignment, I was determined to finish high school. I wasn't about to let my circumstances dictate my future. Within a couple of weeks of arriving in Korat, I signed up for the GED test. I hadn't taken a prep course, and I had no idea if I was truly prepared, but I pushed forward anyway. To my relief, I passed. My educational advisor encouraged me to send the results to my former high school, and soon after, I was awarded a Boscobel High School diploma. It was a major milestone, but I didn't stop there. Over the course of my 5 ½ years in the military, I managed to complete two years of college coursework, steadily working toward a better future.

About a month after settling into my new duty station, my supervisor invited me to his home for a BBQ. I had no idea that a simple meal would change the course of my life forever.

That's where I met my wife, Ms. Sununt "Sue" Benjarong. From the moment I saw her, I knew there was something special about her. She was graceful, intelligent, and had a warmth that immediately drew me in. In a foreign land that still felt unfamiliar, she made me feel at home. We spent time together whenever we could, learning about each other's cultures, dreams, and values. Four months later, without a doubt in my mind, we were married.

Sue was from Mae Chan, Thailand. The Buddhist Temple was less than adequate so in 2017, Sue and I built this temple and donated it to the community.

Our happiness was soon tempered by reality. My military discharge was just a couple of months away, and I knew the bureaucratic nightmare that came with securing a visa for Sue. I quickly realized that if I wanted to ensure our future together, I needed to reenlist for another three years. It wasn't an easy decision, but it was the only option that made sense. I picked up the phone and called my mother to share both my joy and my decision.

She wasn't upset that I had married Sue—she was upset that I had chosen to reenlist. "Please don't reenlist," she pleaded. "Bring Sue home." I understood her concerns. She had already spent years apart from me, and the thought of another three years was difficult to accept. But once I explained the visa situation and the time it would take, she eventually came to terms with it. Still, that didn't make it

14

any easier to accept that another three years would pass before I would return to the States with my bride.

Sue finally received her visa, and it felt like a small victory. But before we could celebrate, a reduction in forces in Thailand led to my reassignment to Hawaii. By then, Sue was four months pregnant, and we were faced with a new challenge—we didn't have the $600 needed for her plane ticket. With no other option, I had to leave her behind.

Hawaii, however, turned out to be a blessing in disguise. As the headquarters for Southeast Asia, it gave me a unique advantage. As soon as I arrived, I wasted no time. I went straight to the military personnel office, explained my situation, and pleaded my case. Within a month, my persistence paid off, and I was issued orders to return to Bangkok. The relief I felt was immeasurable.

Knowing the financial strain we were under, I had arranged for my paycheck to be sent to Sue through the Red Cross. By the time I landed in Thailand, I had about $10 in my pocket. I still had to get to Korat, retrieve Sue and our belongings, and return to Bangkok. My first words upon seeing her weren't "Hi, how are you?" or "I missed you." Instead, they were, "Do you have any money?"

Thankfully, she had saved most of what I had sent! We were able to pay for a taxi from Bangkok to Korat and still had enough left to make the move back to the city. The relief was overwhelming, but it was just another reminder of how resilient and resourceful we had to be to make this work.

We were lucky to have friends in Bangkok who helped us find a home right away. The only problem? It was about a mile from the nearest taxi service. I hadn't even considered how we'd manage transportation, but Sue had. Without telling me, she sold her wedding ring and bought me a motorcycle. I was stunned. In that moment, I realized the true essence of marriage—it's not just about love. It's about partnership, sacrifice, and finding a way forward together. Sue had cemented that lesson for me in the most profound way possible, showing me that true love isn't just about words—it's about action, trust, and unwavering support for one another.

The Power of Partnership: How Marriage Shapes Character and Changes Lives

Our journey was just beginning, and I knew there would be more challenges ahead. But with Sue by my side, I was ready for whatever came next.

In my opinion, if compromise is not achieved, a marriage will not succeed. Relationships are built on give and take, on mutual understanding, and on the ability to recognize that success is rarely an individual effort. Those who believe they made it entirely on their own are not being honest with themselves. Throughout our journey, people have recognized something in Sue and me that we may not have seen in ourselves. They have presented us with opportunities—challenges that required personal sacrifices and commitments. It was always our choice whether to seize them or not. Generally, we accepted these opportunities, even when they seemed daunting. In time, this mutual collaboration and trust in each other allowed us to get ahead. Our marriage has been a testament to the power of unity, resilience, and faith in one another.

I've always believed that strong relationships—especially a strong marriage—can change the direction of a man's life. And the more I've looked into it, the more I've seen that belief backed up by research.

There's compelling evidence that marriage, particularly a healthy and supportive one, plays a powerful role in keeping men out of trouble—including out of prison. Economists and sociologists have studied this for years. One study by the National Bureau of Economic Research found that married men are significantly less likely to commit crimes, especially violent or property crimes. It makes sense: when a man is bonded to someone he loves and feels responsible for, he's far less likely to risk losing it all.

One of the most eye-opening studies I came across was from Laub and Sampson, who tracked delinquent boys for decades. They found that many of these young men, who started out on rough paths, turned their lives around when they got married. But not just any marriage—a stable, emotionally supportive one. These weren't just marriages on paper. They were partnerships that gave these men purpose, accountability, and hope.

I've also seen how this plays out for men returning home from prison. The Urban Institute did a study that showed just how critical family support is. In fact, 70% of formerly incarcerated men said that family—not programs, not parole officers—was the most important factor in staying out of prison. And when that family support came in the form of a spouse who believed in them, it made an even bigger difference.

It's not just about wearing a ring. It's about the emotional bond, the commitment, and the sense that someone is counting on you. That kind of connection can pull a man away from bad decisions and help him build a better life.

So no, marriage isn't a magic cure—but it's a powerful anchor. In a world where so many men feel unmoored, it can be the thing that steadies them and keeps them moving forward.

Life, Duty, and Resilience: Navigating Parenthood and Policing in a Foreign Land

Living in Bangkok was a new adventure, filled with uncertainties, concerns, and, at times, fear. The anticipation of our first child brought with it an overwhelming sense of responsibility. How would I support a family? Could we make it on our own, so far from home? How would we survive? These thoughts kept me awake many nights, making me question whether I was truly ready for this next phase of life. But then, I would look at Sue—calm, steadfast, and unwavering in her belief that we would make it through together.

Sue has always had a remarkable ability to remain present in the moment, focusing on what we had rather than what we lacked. She saw clarity where I saw uncertainty, solutions where I saw problems. Her practical and commonsense approach to life has been one of our greatest strengths. From the very beginning of our relationship, she understood that as long as we had each other, we would find a way to endure.

The challenges we faced were not just emotional, but practical as well. Living in a foreign country meant adjusting to a new culture, language, and way of life. We had to navigate unfamiliar systems, learn the local customs, and find ways to integrate ourselves into the community. Bangkok was vibrant and full of energy, but it could also be overwhelming. The heat, the crowded streets, the different pace of life—it all took some getting used to. Despite these hurdles, we found ways to adapt. We relied on each other more than ever, recognizing that our shared experiences were shaping us into a stronger team. Every challenge was a lesson, every success a shared victory.

Assigned to a Military Police Unit, I found myself navigating a new and challenging environment. Three months into my service, I was promoted to Sergeant, and soon after, I was designated to work alongside the Thai Police in a Crime Suppression Unit. Our primary duty was to patrol the bustling nightlife of Bangkok, monitoring the areas most frequented by troops on rest and relaxation from Vietnam. The job, for the most part, was straightforward, and I encountered few serious problems. However, there were occasions when alcohol took control of an individual's actions, leading to potential trouble. In those instances, my priority was to protect, not to punish. I would escort them to the Military Police station and secure them for the evening. Naturally, they would be upset at first, but when morning came, and they realized no formal behavioral report had been filed, they were immensely grateful. My goal was always to ensure that these soldiers could enjoy their much-needed R&R without making decisions that might jeopardize their futures. .

One of the most valuable lessons I learned during this time was the importance of discretion and judgment. Not every situation required a strict application of the rules; sometimes, it was more beneficial to exercise patience and understanding. The soldiers we encountered were often exhausted, emotionally strained, and in need of a break from the pressures of war. They weren't bad people—they were simply human, dealing with stress in the best way they knew how. By taking a measured approach, I was able to diffuse situations before they escalated, ensuring the safety of the soldiers and maintaining the peace in the areas we patrolled. This experience reinforced my belief that leadership isn't just about authority—it's about responsibility, empathy, and knowing when to intervene and when to step back.

Chapter 2

Returning Stateside

It had been over three years since I last saw my family in Wisconsin. Life in Thailand had been good to me—married with a child, I was happy, but the weight of responsibility was undeniable. My days were filled with duty, and my nights were spent thinking about what the future held for us. With only three months left before rotating out of Thailand, I found myself wondering where my next assignment would be. I hoped to be stationed stateside, but there was no telling where I'd be sent. The thought of another overseas assignment weighed heavily on my mind, and I longed for the familiar comforts of home. A friend, sensing my apprehension, suggested I call the assignment branch at the Pentagon to find out my next station.

At first, I thought he was crazy. Who calls the Pentagon and asks for their assignment? It seemed far-fetched, almost laughable, but the more I thought about it, the more I realized I had nothing to lose. My friend, a government telephone operator, even made the call for me. Before I knew it, I was connected with the right department, and with a deep breath, I identified myself and inquired about my next assignment.

"You'll be returning to Germany," came the response.

My heart sank. I had already served in Germany before my time in Vietnam, and I had no desire to go back. While Germany was not the worst place to be stationed, it wasn't where I wanted to take my family next. I hesitated for a moment, debating whether to push back, and then with nothing to lose, I spoke up.

"I've already spent time in Germany, and I'd really prefer not to return."

To my surprise, the voice on the other end asked, "Where would you like to go?"

I hadn't expected that question, and for a brief second, I was caught off guard. My mind raced. I knew I wanted to be closer to home. Thinking fast, I blurted out, "Armed Forces Police in Chicago, Illinois."

"There are no vacancies in Chicago," he said. "Would Milwaukee be acceptable?"

Milwaukee was only about 150 miles from my hometown of Boscobel. The thought of being that close to home, close enough to visit family regularly, was too good to pass up. Without hesitation, I answered, "Absolutely!"

I was assured my orders would arrive within 30 days. Even then, I couldn't quite believe it. The idea that a single phone call had changed my fate seemed surreal. Until those papers were in my hands, I wouldn't sleep a full night. But when they finally arrived, relief washed over me.

In July of 1972, we boarded a plane in Bangkok, Thailand, heading for Chicago. The plan was simple—our family would meet us at the airport and then drive us to my hometown. Sue, our daughter Marsha, and I were all excited for the journey.

Our first stop was Anchorage, Alaska. It was supposed to be just another routine stop, but two hours before landing, something went terribly wrong—Marsha developed a high fever and went into convulsions.

Panic gripped me as I watched my baby girl struggle. My mind raced with fear and helplessness, but by the grace of God, there was a physician on board. He acted quickly, using ice packs to stabilize her temperature. The tension on the flight was palpable as everyone watched with concern. When we landed in Anchorage, an ambulance was waiting to take us to the hospital.

As we sped toward the hospital, the ambulance driver received a radio message instructing him to return to the airport. We had yet to clear customs or immigration. I held my breath, bracing for the worst, but then the driver made a choice I will never forget—he turned off the radio and said, "We're going to the hospital."

Marsha was closely monitored overnight, and although I was relieved to see her improving, the stress of the journey weighed on me. Meanwhile, I contacted my mother and brother to inform them of our delay. Their voices on the other end of the line reassured me, reminding me that family was waiting. Once she was stable, we cleared customs and continued our journey.

Sue was nervous about meeting my family and wondered how she would be received. She worried about whether she would be accepted, about whether cultural and language barriers would cause awkwardness. I, on the other hand, could hardly wait to see my loved ones again and begin this new chapter with my young family.

When we finally landed in Chicago, the moment I saw my mother, all the miles and years melted away. I held her close, feeling the warmth of home for the first time in years. Sue was still apprehensive, but within minutes, it was as if she and my mother had known each other forever. The warmth and kindness in my mother's eyes reassured Sue in a way that words never could. The four-hour drive to my mother's house was filled with nonstop conversation and laughter. The sound of my family reconnecting, of stories being shared and memories being relived, was music to my ears.

When we arrived, a crowd of family and friends welcomed us. Over the next two weeks of my military leave, my mother's house felt like a revolving door of visitors. Relatives, neighbors, old friends— each person brought with them stories, laughter, and warm embraces.

It was a homecoming in every sense of the word. It became clear that my family was not only accepted but embraced and honored. Sue's nerves disappeared, replaced with warmth and belonging.

Looking back, I can't help but marvel at how everything fell into place. The assignment, the journey, even Marsha's scare—it all led us home. The road ahead was unknown, but for the first time in a long time, I knew we were exactly where we were meant to be.

When we received word that our furniture had arrived from Thailand and was being stored in Milwaukee, Sue and I took advantage of my leave time to secure an apartment. Our daughter Marsha, resilient as ever, stayed with her grandmother. Fortunately, we found suitable housing on the very first day of searching, allowing us to schedule the furniture delivery to coincide with my reporting date for my new assignment. The ease of securing housing was a relief, as transitioning back to life stateside came with its own set of challenges, from adjusting to a new pace of life to managing finances and reestablishing routines.

My new role was with a Military Police Detachment tasked with locating and apprehending military deserters throughout Wisconsin and Michigan's Upper Peninsula. It was demanding work that required a lot of travel, careful coordination, and diligence in locating individuals who, for one reason or another, had chosen to abandon their service commitments. Once taken into custody, they were transported to Waukesha County Jail before being sent to the Great Lakes Naval Station for administrative processing. Most of them received a general discharge under honorable conditions, but each case carried its own story, its own set of circumstances. Some deserters had simply cracked under the pressure of military life, while others had more complicated personal reasons. The work was eye-opening, giving me insight into the struggles and decisions people faced in the service.

By Percy Pitzer

From Battlefield to Badge: Why Veterans See Law Enforcement as a Continuation of Service

For many military veterans returning to civilian life, the choice to pursue a career in law enforcement or corrections is far more than a practical decision—it is a deliberate continuation of a life built on discipline, service, and the defense of societal order. To these individuals, swapping camouflage for a police uniform or correctional officer's attire does not represent a shift in values or identity, but rather a seamless transition from one form of public service to another. The ethos that once guided them through combat zones now anchors them amid the challenges of patrolling city streets, enforcing laws, or maintaining order within prison walls. It is not simply a job they take on, but a mission they carry forward.

This mindset is more than anecdotal—it is actively nurtured and promoted by federal, state, and local agencies across the United States. Recruitment campaigns targeting veterans are widespread and purposeful, drawing on shared language, imagery, and ideals. Agencies like the Department of Veterans Affairs, U.S. Customs and Border Protection, and countless municipal police departments deploy marketing campaigns that emphasize a familiar sense of duty and camaraderie. Common slogans like "Serve Again, in a Different Uniform," "Still Serving, Still Protecting," and "From the Front Lines to the Thin Blue Line" reflect a strategic appeal to those who view service not as a temporary enlistment but a lifelong calling.

Recruitment materials often highlight overlapping skill sets: weapons proficiency, tactical awareness, team leadership, situational control, and mental toughness under stress. A military background is not only welcomed—it is celebrated as a crucial asset. Veterans are reassured that they are stepping into environments where their experience is not just valued, but needed, particularly in roles that demand restraint, rapid decision-making, and physical and psychological resilience.

This targeted recruitment approach has yielded significant

results. According to data from the Bureau of Justice Statistics, about 19 percent of all law enforcement officers in the United States are military veterans. That's nearly one in five officers who have served in the armed forces—an extraordinary figure that speaks to the strong pipeline between the military and law enforcement sectors. These numbers are not coincidental; they reflect both cultural affinity and institutional support for veterans entering public safety roles.

Government policies further reinforce this pathway. Under Veterans' Preference laws, former service members often receive preferential treatment in hiring for federal, state, and municipal jobs. In federal law enforcement, such as with the Federal Bureau of Investigation, Immigration and Customs Enforcement (ICE), and the Federal Bureau of Prisons (BOP), veterans may receive additional points on civil service exams, be eligible for noncompetitive appointments, or qualify for veterans-only job postings. Many agencies allow military time to count toward retirement, offer educational benefits, or even provide specialized training academies geared toward former service members.

Local and state departments frequently follow suit. Police departments in cities like Dallas, San Diego, and Atlanta offer signing bonuses for veterans, accelerated application processing, and educational incentives tied to the GI Bill. Sheriff's offices often reserve a percentage of training academy seats for veterans and collaborate with military transition assistance programs to recruit service members before they formally exit the armed forces. The messaging is clear: "You've served your country; now serve your community."

However, behind the compelling narrative of continued service lies a more complex and sobering reality. Veterans who enter the justice system workforce—whether as police officers, federal agents, or correctional officers—often carry with them the psychological residue of war. Many have experienced combat, witnessed death firsthand, or endured long separations from loved ones. As they transition into civilian roles, they may already be grappling with post-traumatic stress disorder (PTSD), traumatic brain injury, or moral injury—a deep psychological wound resulting from participating in or witnessing acts that contradict one's sense of morality.

In many cases, these existing wounds are not healed by their new roles; they are aggravated. The environments veterans enter—especially in corrections and urban policing—can be cauldrons of secondary trauma. In correctional facilities, officers are routinely exposed to violence, despair, chronic underfunding, and human degradation. They may witness suicides, assaults, riots, and the emotional unraveling of incarcerated individuals. In urban law enforcement settings, they face violent crime, community mistrust, high-pressure confrontations, and frequent moral ambiguity. Rather than finding solace or structure, veterans often find themselves entrenched in new battlefields, ones that exact a slower but equally punishing toll.

This cumulative trauma—trauma upon trauma—can have profound effects. Studies have shown that law enforcement officers and correctional staff experience elevated rates of PTSD, depression, substance abuse, and suicide, with veterans in these roles particularly vulnerable. The compounding of military trauma with justice system trauma creates a cycle that is difficult to break and often goes under-recognized. Institutional support for mental health in these fields is improving but remains insufficient in many jurisdictions, especially in rural or under-resourced departments.

Part of the difficulty lies in the stark contrast between military and justice system cultures. In the military, structure is paramount. Clear chains of command, rigorous training, logistical consistency, and a strong sense of unit cohesion define the work environment. There is typically a shared mission and purpose, supported by a robust network of services: chaplains, medical units, counselors, and peer support systems. In comparison, the justice system—especially corrections—is often chaotic, disorganized, and underfunded. Staffing shortages, mandatory overtime, aging infrastructure, and lack of mental health resources create high-stress environments with little relief. In such conditions, the tight unit cohesion veterans relied on in the military may be absent. The moral clarity of a combat mission can be replaced by ethically murky decisions involving use of force, treatment of inmates, or enforcement of controversial laws.

This dissonance can be jarring. Veterans who anticipated a smooth transfer of skills may find themselves isolated, morally conflicted, and unsupported. Some burn out quickly and leave the profession; others suffer silently, internalizing their struggles out of fear of appearing weak or disloyal. Yet many persist—driven by a core identity rooted in service and sacrifice. They continue to show up for their shifts, mentor younger colleagues, and advocate for reforms that make the system more humane and resilient.

Organizations that succeed in supporting veteran officers often do so by replicating some of the structures in which veterans thrived: clear expectations, strong peer networks, and robust access to behavioral health care. Peer mentoring programs, trauma-informed leadership training, and confidential counseling services are essential tools in helping veterans navigate the unique pressures of law enforcement and corrections.

Ultimately, the convergence of military and law enforcement cultures presents both an opportunity and a challenge. Veterans bring to the table a wealth of experience, strength, and moral clarity. But they also bring vulnerabilities that must be acknowledged and supported. Recognizing the dual nature of their journey—from battlefield to beat, from combat zone to prison corridor—is critical in building a justice system that honors not only their service, but also their humanity.

In doing so, we can ensure that the call to serve, which led them into one uniform and then another, is not a path that leads to quiet suffering—but one that continues to reflect the dignity, purpose, and resilience they have already proven they possess.

Hard Lessons and Lasting Values: Rising Through the Ranks in a Demanding System

To supplement our income, I took on a second job stocking shelves at Kohl's food store from 9:00 PM to 1:00 AM. The extra money wasn't much, but in those days, every penny counted. Working nights after a full day of military duties was exhausting, but I was determined to provide for my family. Sleep was often sacrificed, and I would get home in the early morning hours, rest for a bit, and then be up and ready for my primary duties. Despite the challenges, I took pride in the effort—it was all part of ensuring stability for Sue and Marsha.

With about three months remaining in my 5 ½-year military obligation, I was seriously considering making it a career. The structured environment, the camaraderie, and the sense of duty had shaped my identity. However, during my work, I crossed paths with a sheriff in central Wisconsin who mentioned a new federal prison opening in Oxford. He was contemplating leaving his position to seek employment there.

I shared that I was close to military discharge and was interested in the opportunity myself. He dismissed my chances, stating they were only looking for individuals with prior experience. His words stung. I had spent years honing my skills in military law enforcement and security roles—was that not experience? The more I thought about it, the more determined I became. That conversation solidified my decision to leave the military and pursue a career with the Federal Bureau of Prisons.

Back in Milwaukee, I spent hours working the phones to identify job openings within the Bureau of Prisons. My persistence paid off when I discovered that the Federal Correctional Institution in Milan, Michigan was hiring. Without hesitation, I applied, interviewed, and secured the job. I was officially discharged from the military on a Wednesday and, the following Monday, December 9, 1973, I started my new career as a correctional officer. It was a whirlwind transition, barely giving me time to process the change, but I was grateful for the opportunity. The first two weeks of my new job were spent in training. I was nervous, apprehensive, and maybe even a little scared. I had left a stable job, moved my entire family, and entered the unknown. What if I failed? Would I have to return to the military? However, I quickly realized that the Bureau of Prisons was invested in my success. The training was rigorous but thorough, equipping me with the knowledge and tools necessary to handle the responsibilities of the job. The instructors emphasized the importance of composure, decision-making, and understanding inmate behavior. It became clear that if I failed, it would be because I didn't take full advantage of the opportunity.

After completing training, I was assigned as a housing unit officer. Again, I felt some apprehension, but I was fortunate to be paired with an excellent senior officer mentor. His guidance, patience, and willingness to answer my endless questions were instrumental to my success in that first year. The work itself was unlike anything I had experienced before. Managing inmates required a mix of authority, respect, and keen observation. Every interaction had the potential to escalate, and I learned quickly that maintaining order required both firmness and fairness. Financially, things remained tight—my wage was $4.37 per hour—but I took every overtime opportunity available, knowing that every extra hour worked meant a bit more security for my family.

Near the end of my first year in Milan, I requested a transfer to FCI Oxford to be closer to my hometown. My request was granted, and we relocated. Both Milan and Oxford had solid correctional professionals, and I settled in well. The work remained demanding, but I was growing into my role and gaining confidence in my ability to handle challenges. However, towards the end of my second year at Oxford, we faced a family crisis. Our five-year-old daughter Marsha was hospitalized with pneumonia. The hospital was 40 miles from home, and Sue did not drive at the time. I requested a day off to be with them, but my supervisor denied it, arguing that since she was receiving medical care, there was no need for me to be there. His

By Percy Pitzer

response felt cold and impersonal. Marsha was young, scared, and needed both of her parents by her side. Sue, unable to get to the hospital on her own, was just as distressed.

As I stood there, frustrated and concerned, the Warden happened by and asked what the issue was. I explained the situation. Without hesitation, he simply said, "Take whatever time you need." His immediate and humane response reinforced my respect for good leadership. It was a moment that stuck with me—one that reminded me of the kind of leader I hoped to be one day.

Thankfully, Marsha fully recovered. However, my supervisor was unhappy with being overruled in the "time off" matter and began making my work at Oxford increasingly difficult. Recognizing the need for a change, I reached out to a friend who had previously transferred from Oxford to FCI-Miami and asked if he could assist me with a transfer. Not only did he help, but I was also transferred with a promotion to Senior Officer Specialist. I want to emphasize that my experience with my Oxford supervisor was not typical—he must have been having a bad day. However, the situation taught me valuable lessons about leadership, particularly in how I would handle authority and personnel matters in the future. I learned that leadership is not about exerting power over others but about creating an environment where employees feel supported and motivated to perform at their best. This experience solidified my belief in fairness, transparency, and treating people with dignity, no matter the circumstances.

After approximately 18 months at FCI-Miami, I was unexpectedly promoted to Lieutenant at the Metropolitan Correctional Center (MCC) in New York City—one of the busiest facilities in the Bureau of Prisons. Given my experience as a shift supervisor in the military, I believed I was well-versed in leadership. Yet, within a short period, I realized I had much more to learn. My new role exposed me to situations I could have never imagined, testing my adaptability and decision-making skills in ways I had never encountered before.

One of the biggest challenges at MCC was the fast-paced nature of the job. The volume of incidents, the complexity of the inmate population, and the constant movement of detainees from court to facility and back again created an environment where officers had to be sharp, decisive, and always prepared. I encountered high-profile criminals, individuals with powerful connections, and some who had spent their entire lives in and out of institutions. Learning how to manage a facility that housed such a diverse group of inmates required me to refine my leadership skills daily.

Initially, I took the approach that the more I identified "wrong"— specifically, instances of non-compliance—the better I could lead. However, I quickly realized that focusing on what was "right," while also addressing necessary changes, garnered more support and cooperation from staff. This experience taught me an essential leadership lesson: Involve staff in decision-making whenever possible. Empowering employees fosters a more effective and collaborative work environment. I began to see leadership in a new light—one that valued input, acknowledged strengths, and guided employees toward collective success rather than just pointing out shortcomings. Over time, I found that treating my staff with respect and including them in key decisions not only improved morale but also enhanced operational efficiency.

Life in New York City was incredibly expensive. Unfortunately, MCC staff did not receive a high cost-of-living allowance, making financial survival a challenge. Sue and I had to rely on overtime, and she even took a job cleaning banks to help make ends meet. It was frustrating to realize that at the time, a garbage collector made more than a correctional officer. This is not to demean the importance of sanitation workers—we need a clean environment—but rather to highlight the stark disparity in compensation for those responsible for maintaining security and order in a correctional setting. Staffing shortages and fair salary compensation have been longstanding issues in the Bureau of Prisons.

The financial strain affected not only us but also many of my colleagues. Some officers took second jobs, while others shared apartments far outside the city to save on rent. There was little room for luxury or financial stability despite the demanding nature of our work. Many correctional officers, including myself, were left questioning why those in charge failed to acknowledge the financial struggles of those maintaining law and order.

After a year at MCC, I was promoted to Senior Lieutenant. The pay increase helped slightly, but we continued to struggle financially in New York. Then, in November of 1979, I received a call that my mother was gravely ill, and I needed to return home to Wisconsin immediately. We had a choice—pay the rent or purchase plane tickets for the family. The decision was obvious: We bought the tickets and returned to Wisconsin. Within an hour of arriving at my mother's bedside, she passed away. It felt as if she had waited for our presence before departing this world. While we were deeply saddened by our loss, we were grateful to have been with her in her final moments.

Upon our return to New York, we had barely been home for a couple of hours when the landlord knocked on our door, demanding rent. We had never been late before, but he was unsympathetic to our situation. Every day for a month, he stood at our door until the rent was paid. That experience profoundly impacted Sue and me—we made a commitment to each other that if we were ever in a landlord-type position, we would treat people with respect and empathy, understanding their unique circumstances. We saw firsthand how financial difficulties could strike even the most responsible individuals and how a little compassion could go a long way.

Most of my time at MCC was spent as an investigative supervisor. During my 2 ½ years there, nine staff members were indicted for corruption, including a Catholic priest. Before his indictment, I had spoken with him, warning that he was getting too close to a particular organized crime inmate. He took offense and insisted that the inmate was a true gentleman. Eight of the nine indicted staff members ended up serving prison sentences. The priest was banned from the priesthood and faced additional disciplinary actions from the church.

Investigations at MCC were complex and often politically

charged. Corruption within correctional institutions is a difficult issue to address because it stems from multiple factors—low pay, the influence of high-profile inmates, and the everyday pressures of working in such a stressful environment. Many of those who succumbed to corruption never set out to break the law, but the gradual erosion of ethical boundaries, combined with financial stress and manipulation from inmates, led them down a dangerous path. Seeing colleagues, people I had once trusted, end up on the wrong side of the law was disheartening. It reinforced the importance of integrity and the need for better oversight and support for correctional staff.

One may ask why the Bureau of Prisons did not take stronger action to address these growing concerns. Compensation issues plagued not just NYC but correctional institutions across the country. Corruption was on the rise. The answer is simple: the agency had to work with the limited resources provided. Politicians frequently push "tough on crime" policies, yet they fail to adequately fund the true cost of incarceration. Whether due to ignorance or indifference, they do not grasp the struggles correctional professionals endure due to inadequate financial compensation. Addressing this issue through education and policy reform is imperative and long overdue.

Chapter 3

Foundations of Leadership: From Construction to Crisis

I n 1980, I was transferred from the Metropolitan Correctional Center in New York City to the Federal Correctional Institution (FCI) in Otisville, New York. This transfer was a relief for my family, as the cost of living in Otisville was significantly lower than in New York City. Otisville was so new at the time that construction on the facility had not yet been completed. Shortly after my arrival, designated minimum-security inmates were brought in to help finish the construction. Some staff members were tasked with developing policies and procedures, while the rest of us worked alongside inmates to complete the construction project. It wasn't long before the facility was fully operational, though the early days were filled with challenges.

Working in a facility still under construction was a unique experience. Many of us had to adapt to an ever-changing environment, as policies were being drafted at the same time that walls were being painted and floors laid down. There was a certain camaraderie in those early days, as staff and inmates alike worked toward the same goal—getting Otisville up and running as a fully operational institution. It was an era when correctional philosophy was beginning to shift toward rehabilitation, and I found it inspiring to be part of something that aimed to return people to society better than they arrived.

The warden at Otisville was J. Michael Quinlan, who later became the Director of the Bureau of Prisons. He was an innovative and creative leader who believed that an inmate's punishment was the sentence itself. He emphasized that the role of a correctional institution was to prepare inmates for successful reintegration into society. His philosophy included providing educational programs and skill-building opportunities, with mental health support as a critical component. His leadership style made a lasting impression on me, reinforcing my belief that true corrections should focus not just on confinement but also on transformation.

Throughout my 25-year career with the BOP, I had the privilege of working under several wardens, each of whom taught me valuable lessons. I was particularly fortunate to serve under three exceptional Directors: Norman Carlson, J. Michael Quinlan, and Kathleen Hawk-Sawyer. Their leadership was exemplary, and I would have walked through fire for any one of them because I knew they would have found a way to get me out. They consistently demonstrated solid correctional practices, embodying true leadership. Their ultimate goal was to ensure that people reentered the community better equipped to handle life's challenges. Their influence helped shape my own leadership philosophy, which was rooted in fairness, discipline, and a genuine commitment to positive outcomes for both staff and inmates.

Years later, I had the opportunity to sit down with Dan Dove, another former warden who oversaw a medium-security institution in Ashland, Kentucky. Our conversation was an eye-opener on the effectiveness of inmate reform programs and how structured educational and vocational training can reshape lives. It reinforced my belief that incarceration should be about more than just punishment —it should be about transformation and rehabilitation.

Dan explained that at his facility, every inmate who entered and scored a 6.0-grade level or lower was automatically required to enroll in an adult education program. There was no option to refuse. The idea was simple: if an inmate lacked basic literacy or numeracy skills, they wouldn't stand a chance at finding gainful employment post-release. For those who scored above that threshold but still lacked a high school diploma, the opportunity to pursue their GED was readily available. Many inmates took this path and left prison with a diploma in hand, something they had never achieved in their lives outside. The goal was to ensure that no inmate left the institution without at least some form of foundational education, setting them up for success instead of recidivism.

Beyond secondary education, Dan's facility offered a community college program within the prison walls. Inmates could apply for Pell Grants, which provided them with the financial support needed to take college courses while incarcerated. This initiative not only expanded their educational horizons but also improved their chances of securing meaningful employment upon release. Higher education opened doors that otherwise would have remained closed, and many inmates found a sense of purpose they had never experienced before. Some of them pursued associate degrees, and in rare cases, even bachelor's degrees upon release. This type of education was a game-changer, offering inmates not just knowledge but also confidence in their own abilities.

In addition to traditional education, vocational training played a significant role in inmate rehabilitation. Dan's prison offered a variety of vocational programs, including autobody repair, auto mechanics, welding, and a robust federal prison industry initiative. The latter, managed by a central office in Washington, D.C., specialized in woodworking. The woodworking program was a comprehensive operation, ranging from basic cleanup roles to skilled craftsmanship. Inmates created high-quality furniture, much of which was sold to government entities, including executive offices in Washington, D.C.

This program was transformative on multiple levels. Not only did it provide inmates with wages they could use at the commissary or send home to their families, but it also taught them critical life and job skills. Many of these men had never held a steady job before prison, and through these programs, they learned the fundamentals of workforce participation—showing up on time, following instructions, working as a team, and taking pride in their craft. The program also helped inmates develop discipline, patience, and attention to detail—qualities that could serve them well in any future job. Those who already had experience in woodworking honed their skills further, producing intricate furniture that rivaled pieces made in high-end workshops. It wasn't just about teaching them how to use tools; it was about teaching them how to take responsibility for their work and develop a sense of ownership over their contributions.

Dan shared a particularly remarkable story about one inmate who was serving a ten-year sentence. This man had been convicted of murder, though it was classified as a crime of passion and he was a first-time offender. Despite the severity of his crime, he demonstrated an exceptional work ethic in the woodworking program. His skills and dedication were so impressive that the federal prison industries division made an unprecedented request: they asked Dan to authorize this inmate to deliver materials to other federal institutions and prison industry facilities.

Dan was hesitant at first, given the inmate's background, but decided to approve it on a trial basis. The arrangement worked remarkably well. The inmate was placed on single-day furloughs to transport raw and finished materials between five prison industry facilities across Kentucky. He performed this role successfully for several years, proving to be trustworthy and responsible. Over time, he became one of the most reliable workers in the program, gaining the respect of both staff and fellow inmates. His dedication to his work showed that incarceration does not define a person; rather, it is how they respond to their circumstances that matters.

When the time came for his parole hearing, his work history and the skills he had developed in the prison industry program played a major role in securing his release. The parole board recognized his transformation, acknowledging that he had taken full advantage of the rehabilitation programs available to him.

Upon release, the former inmate took his newfound skills and applied them to the outside world. He became a truck driver, a profession that aligned with his passion for travel and movement. Thanks to the training and experience he gained while incarcerated, he was able to build a stable and productive life after prison. He stayed in touch with some of the staff at Ashland, expressing gratitude for the opportunities he had been given and sharing updates on his career. His story was a testament to the fact that with the right support and training, even those who have made serious mistakes can turn their lives around.

Listening to Dan recount this story reinforced my belief in the importance of true inmate reform. Education, vocational training, and work programs are not just about keeping inmates occupied—they are about giving them the tools to rebuild their lives. Dan's experiences at Ashland showed that when given the right opportunities, even those who have made grave mistakes can change their trajectory and contribute meaningfully to society. It's a lesson that should guide correctional institutions everywhere.

As I reflected on our conversation, I couldn't help but think about how many lives could be transformed if every correctional facility adopted similar initiatives. The key to reducing recidivism isn't just locking people away—it's preparing them for life beyond bars. Dan's institution was proof that with the right programs, we could take men who had lost their way and give them a real chance at redemption. And that, in the end, is what true justice should be about.

After a couple of years at Otisville, I received a promotion and was transferred back to Miami as a Unit Manager. The mission of the facility had changed since my initial assignment at FCI-Miami; it had transitioned from housing sentenced inmates to operating as an MCC, primarily housing pretrial detainees. This shift occurred in the mid-1980s due to the surge of drugs entering the United States from South and Central America, with Miami being a major hub. The cartels kept us busy.

Miami was a hotbed of criminal activity at the time, with drug-related violence escalating throughout the city. The influx of high-profile detainees added another layer of complexity to the job. The sheer volume of cases coming through the facility was staggering, and we found ourselves dealing with everything from low-level drug runners to major cartel figures. It was a time of long hours and high stress, but it was also an invaluable learning experience.

During this time, the political landscape shifted toward a "tough on crime" stance, resulting in the construction of more prisons and the imposition of longer sentences. Within the prison system, we knew this would lead to overpopulation, and we were unprepared to handle the anticipated influx. While I have seen many inmates receive life sentences—deservedly so, in many cases—95 percent of incarcerated individuals eventually return to their communities. The critical question remains: Will they live purposeful lives? Have they been given the tools and skills to succeed? Are they ready? I have always believed that "getting smart on crime" is a wiser approach than simply being tough on crime. The policies of the time created massive institutional challenges, with overcrowding placing enormous strain on resources, staff, and rehabilitation programs.

Miami remains one of my favorite places. I have lived in many cities across America, but I have never had better neighbors than Cuban Americans. One morning, I woke to the sound of a lawnmower. Aware that I was struggling with a painful bout of gout and unable to walk, my neighbor had taken it upon himself to mow our lawn. We hadn't asked for help. Another weekend, I was up on a ladder painting the trim on our house when, within two hours, six neighbors showed up with ladders, coolers of food, drinks, and even a grill. Without being asked, they transformed our small painting project into a full weekend effort, repainting the entire house. My wife, Sue, and I were deeply grateful for their generosity and kindness. That spirit of community was something I came to deeply appreciate, and it reinforced my belief in the fundamental goodness of people when given the right opportunities.

MCC-Miami was a great place to work, filled with employees who demonstrated strong work ethics, solid values, and a commitment to doing their jobs well. Like any large organization, we had our share of challenges. One day, an inmate came to my office and claimed that Mr. X was bringing in contraband. I initially dismissed the idea, convinced that Mr. X would never do such a thing. But the inmate was insistent. I ended the conversation by telling him to prove it—by bringing me a Big Mac and an order of fries. Two days later, the inmate walked into my office and placed a Big Mac and fries on my desk. The matter was referred to the FBI, and the individual in question was prosecuted and received supervised probation. That incident reinforced an important lesson: in a prison environment, you must always remain vigilant. Assumptions can be dangerous, and even the most trusted individuals are capable of deception.

I am grateful for my time in Miami, and I am fortunate to have worked in many BOP facilities that upheld exemplary standards.

My next promotion took me to the Control Unit at the United States Penitentiary (USP) in Marion, Illinois. Once again, this required relocation. This high-security facility housed inmates who could not be controlled within the general prison population. Most had committed violent acts, including the murder of fellow inmates or staff members, while incarcerated. Just a few years before my arrival, two staff members were murdered in the Control Unit on the same day by inmates affiliated with the Aryan Brotherhood.

I had concerns about this assignment, as my primary responsibility was to ensure staff safety while overseeing a high-security unit. Initially, the staff was understandably wary of my leadership. They didn't know my management style or what to expect from me. Though my role was to lead, I found that functioning as a team member was the most effective approach. While I questioned some existing policies and procedures at first, I took the time to observe them in practice. Over time, I came to understand their necessity and effectiveness.

My first trip "down range"—where the inmates were housed—was one I won't forget. I was escorted by two staff members, my senses heightened as I stepped into the controlled chaos of the facility. The weight of my new responsibilities pressed against me, but I knew that composure was key. It was essential to establish a presence of authority while maintaining the respect of both the staff and the inmate population.

As we moved through the corridor, an inmate called out, requesting to speak with me. I hesitated only for a moment before approaching his cell, meeting his intense gaze through the bars. Without hesitation, he demanded, "What the fuck are you going to do for me?"

Without missing a beat, I responded, "Not a fucking thing," and continued walking.

That was not my usual way of interacting with inmates, but I sensed he was testing boundaries. My instincts told me that meeting his challenge with equal assertiveness was necessary at that moment. I needed to show that I would not be intimidated or manipulated. It must have been the right move—I never faced another situation like that again.

My nearly two years at USP-Marion were invaluable. The team-work among staff was unwavering. We trusted one another, knowing that maintaining a safe environment depended on our collective effort. The professionalism and dedication I witnessed daily rein-forced my belief in the power of strong leadership and cohesion. The job was intense, requiring constant vigilance and adaptability, but the camaraderie among the staff made all the difference.

Eventually, I received a transfer and promotion to Associate Warden at La Tuna FCI in Anthony, Texas, a lower-security facility just outside El Paso. Moving from a maximum-security prison to this setting was a welcomed change. At Marion, the envi-ronment was always tense, with the potential for violence looming just beneath the surface. La Tuna, in contrast, felt more like a place of rehabilitation. I quickly recognized that the leadership at La Tuna was solid and forward-thinking. The institution prioritized training and education programs for inmates while fostering positive community relations. There was a clear understanding that incarceration alone was not a solution—it had to be accompanied by efforts to prepare inmates for successful reintegration into society.

However, I understood that even the best programs wouldn't make a lasting impact if former inmates were released into communities unprepared for their reintegration. Many ended up in prison simply because they never knew another way of life—trapped in cycles of poverty, addiction, or crime. Without external support, they would often fall back into the patterns that landed them behind bars in the first place. Women, in particular, often found themselves controlled by abusive partners or exploitative organizations. Their involvement in criminal activities was frequently not of their own volition but a matter of survival or coercion. Breaking these cycles required more than just prison reform; it demanded education, support, and structured guidance both inside and outside prison walls.

A clear example of our commitment to community engagement took place one Thanksgiving when we provided 2,500 meals to the town's 3,500 residents. Staff, inmates, and community members came together to make it happen, proving that collaboration benefited everyone. The effort went beyond just feeding people—it demonstrated how correctional facilities could play a positive role in the surrounding community. It was one of those moments that reminded me why I had chosen this career in the first place.

Another moment that stands out was when a local police officer was killed in the line of duty. The department requested donations for bulletproof vests, and I proposed involving the inmates. At first, their response was outright rejection, laced with colorful language about how the police were responsible for putting them behind bars.

Their hostility was understandable—many of them had personal grievances against law enforcement.

I countered by asking them a simple question: "If the Aryan Brotherhood or the Black Gangster Disciples were the ones responding to your family's emergencies, would you feel safer? Or would you prefer it to be the police?"

That shift in perspective changed everything. They ended up donating $3,000 to the vest fund. Time and again, I learned that when you provide people with a rational explanation, most—regardless of their background—respond with common sense and decency.

After three years at La Tuna, I was transferred back to Miami for a third time. I arrived in August 1992, and within weeks, I faced a situation I had never prepared for—Hurricane Andrew. A Category 5 storm with sustained winds of 165 mph was barreling toward us. Neither I nor most of the staff had any experience with hurricanes, but we did our best to prepare. Disaster preparedness had never been a primary focus in our training, and we were about to learn firsthand how critical it was.

At the time, my wife Sue and I were still in temporary housing, so I had her come to the institution, thinking she would be safer there. In hindsight, she probably would have been safer in our temporary housing. The storm's unpredictability made every decision a gamble, and the reality of the situation didn't truly set in until the wind started howling through the facility.

The Warden set up in the command center outside the prison perimeter, while I was the operations officer inside. As the storm began to hit, I drove the perimeter to check on the patrol officers. The wind was so powerful that the front end of my vehicle lifted off the ground. That's when I knew we were in serious trouble. I immediately ordered an evacuation of those posts and secured the inmates in their cells to prevent chaos. The last thing we needed was a panicked prison population reacting to the storm's destruction.

With my team, I took shelter in the control center, maintaining what little communication we had. The devastation was unlike anything I had ever seen—light poles crashing onto buildings, trees ripped from the earth, vehicles tossed like toys. The perimeter fence was completely obliterated. If we hadn't secured the inmates beforehand, the situation could have spiraled into absolute disaster.

I contacted the Regional Office to recommend an immediate evacuation of the inmates once the storm passed. Right as I was speaking, we lost communication. For two long hours, I had no idea if they had received my message. When contact was restored, I was relieved to learn that my request had been understood. Transportation was already on standby, and within hours of the storm clearing, the facility was safely evacuated.

Despite the catastrophic conditions, we managed to get through Hurricane Andrew without a single staff or inmate injury. That was only possible because of the selfless teamwork and unwavering dedication of our staff. I will forever be grateful for their resilience and commitment during one of the most challenging moments of my career. In the years that followed, I carried the lessons learned from that experience—about leadership, crisis management, and the unbreakable strength of teamwork—with me through every challenge that came my way.

Chapter 4

A Warden's Journey: From High Security to No Security

I n mid-1995, I was promoted to Warden and transferred to the Federal Prison Camp (FPC) in Duluth, Minnesota. Having spent most of my career in mid-to-high security institutions, adjusting to a minimum-security prison was a significant change. There were no fences, no doors on the cells, and essentially no security measures as I had known them. To be honest, it was a culture shock.

Before my arrival, an official from the Bureau of Prisons called me with a bit of advice. He said, "Where you're headed is not a penitentiary. I suggest that upon arrival you meet the staff, return to your office, sit at your desk, and read the newspaper." He went on to say, "Once a week, make rounds, return to your office, and read more newspapers." He was exaggerating, of course, but not by much. The Duluth FPC population was around 450 inmates, a far cry from my previous assignments. The inmates worked, attended programs, and the facility ran smoothly—a stark contrast to what I was used to.

On my first day, as I sat at my desk, I noticed paperwork for a disciplinary action against a staff member. The proposal was a one-day suspension without pay for getting his truck stuck near the perimeter fence. This fence was not for security but to delineate the facility's boundary from the surrounding community. I called the employee in and asked him why it happened. His response? "To prevent inmates from escaping." I asked him why an inmate would climb over the fence rather than simply walk around it. When he didn't have an answer, I suggested he practice common sense in the future. No disciplinary action was taken.

My time at Duluth FPC allowed me to reflect on the broader implications of how we managed minimum-security inmates. At that time, the BOP budget was estimated for 24,000 FPC inmates at an average cost of $152.02 per inmate per day, totaling approximately $1.3 billion annually. And that didn't even include the additional costs of family members who might require public assistance due to an incarcerated breadwinner. Given such an immense budget, it made sense to explore alternatives for minimum-security inmates. Home confinement, electronic monitoring, and community supervision could allow inmates to work, support their families, and reduce the burden on taxpayers. The reality was that many of these inmates did not need to be in a facility at all. If an inmate violated their conditions, they could simply be returned to a low-security facility. This is precisely why we need to be smart on crime rather than just tough on crime. We can do better.

One of the most eye-opening aspects of working in a minimum-security environment was the level of trust inherent in the system. These were inmates who, in many cases, had made mistakes that did not warrant severe confinement. They had structure and responsibilities within the facility, and many of them were deeply motivated to complete their sentences and reintegrate into society. It was a stark contrast from my previous experiences where constant vigilance was necessary to maintain control and security. In Duluth, it was more about management than enforcement. The inmates were largely self-governing, with work assignments and programs that gave them a purpose.

After 18 months at FPC Duluth, I called my Regional Director,

Pat Kane, and requested a transfer. When he asked why, I told him I was bored and cold. He chuckled and asked where I wanted to go. "Anywhere south," I replied. A couple of weeks later, he called back with good news and bad news. The good news? I was being transferred. The bad news? My next assignment was at FCI Oxford in Wisconsin. It wasn't quite the warm climate I had hoped for, but I was honored that Pat wanted to keep me in his region. Pat was a true leader and, sadly, passed away from cancer at an early age.

Returning to Oxford was a unique experience. I had worked there as a young correctional officer and now I was returning as Warden. I wondered how the staff who remembered me would perceive me. As it turned out, I was received as the same person in both roles. That kind of consistency in character and reputation was humbling.

Oxford had a long history of being a well-run facility with dedicated staff. But it was also a place of tragedy. On January 29, 1984, correctional officer Boyd Spikerman was bludgeoned to death with a fire extinguisher by an inmate. Even 40 years later, the staff still mourned his loss. It was a sobering reminder of the dangers inherent in this line of work. Boyd's death served as a permanent cautionary tale that even in a well-managed institution, vigilance and preparedness were paramount.

The transition back to a higher-security facility required me to shift my mindset once again. Unlike Duluth, Oxford required more intensive management and security measures. The staff were dedicated and well-trained, and their commitment to maintaining order was evident. I worked closely with them to ensure a safe and structured environment for both staff and inmates. I also took the opportunity to implement some of the lessons I had learned from my time at Duluth—particularly in terms of rehabilitation efforts and alternative strategies for managing low-risk offenders. I had come to realize that many of the blanket policies in place within the BOP could benefit from a more nuanced approach.

Make a Difference with Your Review

Help Others Find Hope and Second Chances

"The best way to find yourself is to lose yourself in the service of others."
– Mahatma Gandhi

Some people give with their time. Others with their heart. Right now, your words can do both.

If this book meant something to you—if it made you think, feel, or see the world a little differently—I'd be grateful if you'd share that. There are people out there who don't know this story yet. **But your review could help them find it**.

You might help:
- one more warden believe in redemption
- one more reader see people in prison as human
- one more second-chance story begin

It costs nothing. Takes just a minute. But it can mean everything to someone on the edge of hope.

Thank you for reading. And thank you for caring.
– Percy Pitzer

To leave a review, just scan the QR code above

Part Two

LEADING

Chapter 5

Leadership, Integrity, and the Evolution of Corrections

As my career with the BOP neared its end, I was transferred to USP Beaumont, Texas. The facility was relatively new, having been activated less than two years prior by Warden Raymond Holt.

He had done an outstanding job hiring top-notch employees and ensuring they received excellent training. His leadership made my transition and role much easier.

USP Beaumont was a high-security facility, a return to the world I had originally come from. It was a challenging environment, but one that I understood well.

I've spent much of my career in corrections, and one thing has become increasingly clear to me: being "tough on crime" may sound good in a soundbite, but it often doesn't make us safer. What we really need is to be *smarter* on crime. That means rethinking how we use our correctional systems—not simply as warehouses for people who've broken the law, but as places where we can actually help change the trajectory of their lives. It's time we shift the conversation toward what works—not what sounds the toughest.

One of the most effective ways to do this is by offering a full range of vocational training, educational programs, substance abuse treatment, and personal development opportunities to sentenced individuals in our jails and prisons. These programs have a proven track record of reducing recidivism, increasing post-release success, and enhancing overall community safety. But this work can't fall solely on the shoulders of correctional staff. The most effective programs I've seen are those supported by actively engaged community volunteers, religious leaders, and faith-based organizations—people and groups who continue to walk alongside individuals after they've served their time. Their role is critical in bridging the gap between incarceration and reintegration.

And here's the key: being smart on crime means recognizing that this isn't just about second chances—it's about public safety, fiscal responsibility, and long-term solutions.

When I served as a warden at the U.S. Penitentiary in Beaumont, I had the opportunity in 1998 to lead the conversion of a standard housing unit into a specialized, residentially based drug treatment unit under the Residential Drug Abuse Program (RDAP). RDAP was the Federal Bureau of Prisons' flagship substance abuse treatment initiative. It was designed as a rigorous, 6–9-month therapeutic community for offenders diagnosed with substance use disorders. The goal was straightforward: to change behavior, reduce relapse, and support long-term reintegration.

At the time, RDAP was mostly being implemented in low- and medium-security prisons. That made sense on paper—those individuals were closer to release and viewed as more "program-ready." But I saw an opportunity to expand its reach to a population that desperately needed it: inmates in high-security penitentiaries. These individuals often had more serious criminal histories and a higher statistical likelihood of reoffending. But if we could intervene early and effectively—even change the course of just a few lives—the impact could be enormous. These were the men who were most likely to return to our communities and cause harm. Helping them succeed wasn't charity—it was strategy.

I sat down with key correctional administrators and made the case. To their credit, they listened. We implemented RDAP in the penitentiary, and the results were encouraging. This wasn't a gamble. This was a calculated investment in public safety.

And two and a half decades of research has since borne this out. Multiple high-quality studies and government reports confirm that RDAP works—and works well. Here's why policymakers should take notice:

1. Substantial Reduction in Recidivism

Let's start with the bottom line: RDAP reduces reoffending. According to the U.S. Sentencing Commission, only 48.2% of RDAP completers recidivated within eight years, compared to 68% of similarly situated individuals who were eligible but did not participate. That's a 27% drop. For every person who doesn't return to prison, we avoid the high costs of prosecution, incarceration, victimization, and law enforcement response.

2. Cost Savings through Early Release

Under 18 U.S.C. § 3621(e), eligible RDAP participants can receive up to 12 months off their sentence. That adds up fast. Think about the per-inmate cost of incarceration—which ranges from $30,000 to over $60,000 per year depending on the facility. Even with an average sentence reduction of eight months, the savings are significant. But more than just the cost benefit, this incentive gives offenders a concrete reason to fully engage with the program. It's a classic example of how good policy can align incentives in a way that benefits both individuals and the system.

3. Improved Institutional Safety

This may not always be front-of-mind for those outside corrections, but for those of us who've managed facilities, it matters; programs like RDAP make prisons safer. When inmates are engaged in structured, therapeutic programming, they're less likely to get involved in violence, contraband, or other disruptive behavior. That improves safety for staff, for other inmates, and for the broader institution. It also reduces the need for costly lockdowns and disciplinary actions.

4. Better Health Outcomes

RDAP uses evidence-based cognitive behavioral therapy (CBT) to address addiction and associated thinking patterns. The result? Better mental health, lower rates of in-prison drug use, and fewer overdoses post-release. When you improve someone's health and stability, you're also improving their ability to work, to parent, to contribute.

5. Stronger Reintegration Outcomes

This may be the most important piece for communities. Individuals who complete RDAP and receive aftercare support upon release are far more likely to stay sober, get jobs, and reconnect with their families. That's how we reduce intergenerational cycles of crime and poverty. These aren't just statistics—these are real families staying together, real children growing up with more stability, and real neighborhoods experiencing less violence.

So, what does this mean for policymakers?

It means that now—more than ever—we need to shift from reactive, punishment-based policies to proactive, evidence-based investments. It means prioritizing treatment and programming as a *core component* of our public safety strategy, not a side project. It means backing up our tough talk on crime with *smart*, data-driven action.

If we truly want to make our communities safer, reduce the tax burden of repeat incarceration, and build a more just and effective criminal justice system, then we must double down on what works. Programs like RDAP aren't luxuries—they're necessities. They reduce crime. They save money. And they save lives.

We need policies that:

- Expand access to RDAP and similar programs across all security levels.

- Fund staffing and facility upgrades that allow for greater program capacity.
- Provide seamless transition and aftercare services in the community.
- Strengthen partnerships between corrections and local organizations.
- Incentivize innovation in correctional programming and evaluation.

We know that locking people up without a plan for rehabilitation doesn't work. But when we equip incarcerated individuals with the tools to change—and we hold them accountable to that change—we set the stage for safer communities and more productive citizens.

After twenty-five years with the BOP, I retired on December 30, 1998. Sue and I were ready to embark on a new chapter in our lives. The years had been demanding, rewarding, and sometimes even bewildering, but I wouldn't have traded them for anything. My experiences had shaped my understanding of the criminal justice system and the need for meaningful reforms. Now, it was time for something new, and I looked forward to whatever lay ahead.

During my tenure with the Bureau of Prisons, I had the privilege of serving under outstanding leadership. The agency placed a strong emphasis on the welfare of its employees, fostering an environment where staff felt valued and supported. It was this culture of care that enabled the BOP to maintain a high level of professionalism and effectiveness. I credit my career longevity not only to the stability and consistency of BOP leadership but also to the unwavering partnership I shared with my wife. Her support was instrumental in the decisions we made throughout my career, giving us the confidence to navigate the challenges and opportunities that came our way. Having a strong foundation at home provided me with the clarity and resilience needed to succeed in such a demanding profession.

For 25 years, the BOP was regarded as the premiere correctional organization in the world. Throughout my service, the agency was led by only three directors, a testament to its strong and consistent leadership. This continuity allowed for a steady progression of policies and improvements, rather than abrupt changes that could disrupt the organization. The BOP was not just respected within the field of corrections but was recognized as a pillar of excellence within the federal government as a whole. It was an agency that others looked to for guidance, whether in correctional management, rehabilitation programs, or security protocols.

After my time with the BOP, my next venture led me to the private corrections sector with Corrections Corporation of America (CCA), now known as CoreCivic. Transitioning from a federal agency to a private prison system was an adjustment, but I was eager to take on new challenges. I was assigned as Warden at the Whiteville, Tennessee facility, which housed inmates from the state of Wisconsin. This assignment came with its own set of challenges, particularly due to the political controversies surrounding private prisons operating for profit and the out-of-state placement of Wisconsin inmates. However, I was not concerned about privatization. The Wisconsin Department of Corrections conducted rigorous audits, scrutinizing the facility even more closely than I had experienced while serving as a Warden in the BOP. Every aspect of operations, from security measures to rehabilitative programs, was under constant review.

Every correctional facility has its share of incidents, and Whiteville was no exception. One day, while making rounds, I noticed a female staff member interacting with a small group of inmates. There was nothing overtly inappropriate about the interaction, but something about it left me uneasy. The feeling lingered with me throughout the day, prompting me to call her into my office the next morning. When I asked about her relationship with the inmates, she assured me that she valued her job and would never jeopardize it by engaging in inappropriate behavior. As our conversation continued, however, she broke down and admitted to an intimate relationship with one of the inmates. Her reasoning was heartbreaking—she confided that her husband mistreated her at home, while the inmates treated her with kindness. Unfortunately, she had fallen victim to manipulation, a common yet tragic occurrence in correctional environments. The discovery cost her the job, serving as a sobering reminder of the vulnerabilities that can exist within prison walls. It was a stark example of how personal struggles could influence professional decisions, and it underscored the importance of strong leadership in maintaining ethical standards.

The CCA facility in Whiteville frequently made headlines in Wisconsin, with politicians criticizing the state's decision to house inmates out of state. I empathized with the families of those incarcerated, knowing that the distance made visitation nearly impossible. This external scrutiny sometimes fueled unrest within the facility. On one occasion, a group of inmate instigators and several followers took control of the food service department, prompting an immediate lockdown. The situation was tense, but within two hours, order was restored, and the inmates responsible were eventually transferred back to Wisconsin. These incidents highlighted the delicate balance required to maintain order in a correctional setting. It was not simply about enforcing rules; it was about understanding human behavior, identifying potential risks, and taking proactive steps to prevent escalations.

After approximately two years at Whiteville, I was transferred to California City, California, where I took on the role of Warden at a 2,500-bed facility designated for sentenced criminal aliens.

By Percy Pitzer

The vast majority—95%—of these inmates were from Mexico and were slated for deportation upon completing their sentences. During my initial tour of the facility, I noticed a large poster in the education department displaying the Declaration of Independence. Given that the inmate population would ultimately return to Mexico, I questioned the relevance of this material. Common sense dictated that the focus should be on education that would benefit these individuals upon their return home, so I had the poster removed.

Recognizing a greater need, I reached out to the Mexican government through their consulate to propose the implementation of a Mexican Education Program within the facility, utilizing a curriculum tailored to their country of origin. They quickly agreed, and through collaboration, we were able to enroll 1,000– 1,500 inmates in a full-time educational program. Inmate tutors, under the supervision of existing staff, played a key role in delivering this instruction. My belief was simple—if we could return these individuals to their home country with an education, they might be less likely to reoffend.

Seeing the success of this initiative, I contacted a high-ranking official in the BOP and suggested they consider adopting a similar program. The response was disappointing but unsurprising: BOP policy required inmates to work for half of each day, which supposedly precluded such a program. My immediate thought was, perhaps it was time to change the policy. Programs like the one we developed provided meaningful engagement for the inmates while contributing to a more orderly and productive facility. The success of our program demonstrated that rehabilitation and education could coexist with operational security.

Despite ongoing debates in the political sphere regarding the ethics of for-profit prisons, I can say with confidence that during my four years with CCA, there was never an instance where I was pressured to cut corners for financial gain. In fact, it would have been nearly impossible to do so, given the extensive oversight from both the Wisconsin Department of Corrections and the Bureau of Prisons. My experiences in both the public and private correctional sectors reinforced my belief in the importance of strong leadership, ethical decision-making, and innovative approaches to rehabilitation. Throughout my career, I remained committed to upholding the highest standards of correctional management while ensuring that those in my charge—both staff and inmates—were treated with fairness and respect. The world of corrections is ever evolving, and while policies and practices may shift, the fundamental principles of integrity and leadership remain constant.

Chapter 6

A Leap of Faith: The birth of Creative Corrections

Sue and I had spent two years in California, but despite the stability of my career, we weren't happy. The long hours, the stress, and the bureaucracy of working as a warden with CCA had taken a toll. I had always been deeply committed to my work, but I had started to feel trapped—like I was just another cog in a massive machine with no control over the direction of my life. We wanted something more. A fresh start. A place where we could pursue a dream instead of just getting by.

That's when Las Vegas, Nevada, entered the picture. It was close enough to California to feel familiar, yet it offered the promise of something new. After much deliberation, we made the decision: we would relocate, leave behind the past, and take a shot at something different. By the first week of January 2003, we had found a home, packed up everything we owned, and made the move. It was exhilarating but terrifying at the same time. I had resigned from my position as Warden, walking away from the security of a steady paycheck and a well-established career. But I wasn't walking into the unknown without a plan.

For years, I had observed a glaring need in the corrections

industry—one that I knew could be turned into an opportunity. Prisons and detention facilities across the country were constantly facing compliance issues, operational inefficiencies, and policy failures, yet there was no standardized system to audit, evaluate, and improve these institutions. My experience had shown me just how critical oversight was, and I believed a company dedicated to prison auditing and consulting could make a real difference. That was the vision that led us to meet with an attorney and establish Creative Corrections, LLC. It was a leap of faith, but one we were willing to take.

The Harsh Reality of Starting a Business

What I quickly learned, however, was just how little I actually knew about starting and running a business. I had spent my entire career working in a system with rigid rules and protocols, but entrepreneurship was a completely different world. The first shock came with the cost—the sheer amount of money required to get a business off the ground was staggering. Then came credibility—just because I had experience in corrections didn't mean people were willing to take a chance on a brand-new company with no track record. And the biggest surprise of all? The politics. Getting contracts and earning trust wasn't just about proving we could do the job; it was about navigating relationships, reputations, and backroom dealings.

On top of that, no one seemed to believe we had a shot at success. Friends, colleagues, even acquaintances—we could see the doubt in their eyes when we talked about our vision. It was discouraging, but we kept moving forward.

Unfortunately, reality caught up with us faster than we expected. We had put nearly everything we had into launching the company, and within months, we were drowning in debt. Our savings dwindled to nothing, and every passing day without income pushed us closer to financial disaster. We needed funding, and we needed it fast.

I applied for a small business loan through Bank of America, hoping it would buy us some time to establish ourselves. When I got the denial notice, it felt like someone had punched me in the gut. I had always been able to provide for my family, and now I was staring at the very real possibility of failure. With no other options, Sue and I scheduled a visit with a bankruptcy attorney to explore what that might look like.

That meeting was one of the most eye-opening experiences of my life. The attorney sat across from us, almost cheerful as he explained how *"great"* bankruptcy was. He laid out how we could wipe our debts clean and start fresh, even offering a payment plan for his fees. It was as if he thought we should be *excited* about the idea.

I walked out of that office knowing one thing for sure: bankruptcy was not an option. I wasn't going to walk away from our dream that easily. We had to find another way.

The Book Salesman Warden

I started thinking outside the box—what immediate needs did prisons have, and how could I fill them? That's when I noticed something many people overlooked: the lack of Spanish-language books available in prisons. With the high number of Hispanic inmates in the system, there was a clear demand, and I realized I could capitalize on it.

On the surface, it seemed like a straightforward business move: identify an underserved market and meet the demand. But this wasn't just about books or money. The roots of the idea stretched back to an experience I had years earlier, one that left a lasting impression on how I viewed education, rehabilitation, and human dignity inside correctional walls.

I remembered years prior when I was transferred to California for what turned out to be a two-year assignment. The prison I managed housed a unique population—primarily undocumented immigrants, many of whom were just waiting for deportation to Mexico. It was a transitory, uncertain space. These men weren't serving long sentences; they were caught in a system that was simply holding them until their removal orders came through. At first, it felt like a holding pen, not a place where anything meaningful could happen.

One day, I was walking the corridors and stopped to observe a class in session. The inmates were quietly listening, flipping through pages of textbooks, taking notes. It looked productive, at least on the surface. But as I listened in, I realized something that struck me as completely illogical—they were learning about the Declaration of Independence. I asked one of the staff, "Why the hell are we teaching them the Declaration of Independence when they're going to be deported to Mexico?" It made no sense. These men weren't going to become U.S. citizens. They weren't going to vote. They weren't going to participate in American civic life. They were going home—back to a country that, for many, they barely knew or had left behind years earlier.

That moment stayed with me. And it got me thinking: what if, instead of giving them an education rooted in a country they were being removed from, we gave them something that would actually serve them where they were going? What if we offered them the chance to get a real education from their home country—an education that could lead to employment, purpose, or even just a fresh start?

I reached out to the Mexican government through the consulate in California and laid out my vision. I asked if they'd be willing to partner with us to create an official Mexican education program inside the prison. My thinking was simple: if we could use the actual curriculum from Mexico, and issue real diplomas from Mexican institutions, these men might go home with more than just the clothes on their backs—they might go back with an education and a sense of direction. Maybe, just maybe, they'd be less likely to return illegally if they had tools to build a future at home.

To my surprise, they said yes.

Together, we created a program that was unprecedented. Out of a population of 2,500 inmates, I had between 1,100 and 1,500 men enrolled full-time in the Mexican education program at any given time. We didn't add a single teacher to the payroll. Instead, we used the materials and curriculum provided by the Mexican education authorities, and I built a tutoring network from within. Inmate tutors —men who had completed parts of the program themselves or who were naturally literate in both Spanish and the subject matter— served as peer instructors, all under the supervision of our existing teaching staff.

It was a powerful thing to witness. The atmosphere changed. Inmates who had never seen themselves as students were suddenly carrying notebooks, discussing essays, and working through math problems. The classroom became a space of pride, not punishment. More importantly, these men were learning in their native language, with content that was culturally relevant and directly tied to the lives they were about to return to. It wasn't just education—it was preparation for reentry on their own terms, in their own land.

Now I found myself exploring ways to generate revenue from the prison system, that entire experience came flooding back. I remembered the demand—the hunger—for materials in Spanish. I remembered how men lit up when they could read something that reflected their culture, their identity, their homeland. There had been so little available to them, yet their appetite was enormous.

Selling Spanish-language books in prison was a built-in market that had been overlooked. This wasn't just a financial opportunity; it was a chance to fill a cultural and educational gap that I knew existed. I'd seen it with my own eyes. Selling these books could meet an urgent need, give incarcerated individuals a connection to their roots, and yes, provide a revenue stream—all at once.

It wouldn't be easy. The logistics, the sourcing, the bureaucracy— none of that was simple. But I knew from my time in California that the interest was real, the benefit was meaningful, and the market was there. What started as a question in a classroom— "Why are we teaching them the Declaration of Independence?"—had evolved into something much larger. It became a vision: to educate, empower, and enrich, even behind prison walls, in a language people could actually understand.

We made the decision to start importing Spanish-language books from Mexico in bulk—lots of 10,000 at a time—and selling them to correctional facilities. Our garage became our warehouse, our office, and our shipping center all in one.

The work was brutal. Las Vegas summers are no joke, and with temperatures soaring to 115 degrees, Sue and I found ourselves sweating through endless hours of unpacking, sorting, and repacking books for shipment. It wasn't the career path I had envisioned for myself, but at that point, survival was the only priority.

Word got around quickly, and soon enough, I had a new nickname in the industry— "The Retired Warden Book Salesman." People used it jokingly, almost as if they were poking fun at me, but I didn't care. Let them laugh. What mattered was that we were staying afloat and still pushing toward our bigger dream.

A Turning Point: Our First Federal Contract

Through everything, I never lost my faith. I'm not the type to preach or wear my beliefs on my sleeve, but I have always believed there was a divine plan. And in July of 2003, something happened that made me wonder if someone really was looking out for us.

We landed our first federal contract with the Federal Detention Trustee's Office—the government entity responsible for overseeing facilities housing U.S. Marshals' prisoners. This was the break we had been waiting for, but there was a problem: we didn't have the funds to pay the auditors we needed to complete the job.

I reached out to four professionals I knew and respected—the best in the business. I laid it all out honestly: I couldn't pay them upfront, but if they were willing to trust me, I would pay them as soon as the company received payment.

Without hesitation, they all agreed.

That moment was a game-changer. The audits were completed successfully, and those same auditors stayed with us for the long haul. Even more importantly, we had proven ourselves. We had delivered on a major contract, and that meant we weren't just surviving—we were building a real company.

One person who played a pivotal role in our journey was Ms. Claudia Hill-Bickham, the Assistant Chief of the Trustee's Office. She understood how critical this contract was to us and provided guidance that made all the difference. I will always be grateful for her support.

Thinking back to those early days, I can see how close we came to losing everything. The move, the debt, the doubt, the heat in that damn garage—it all could have broken us. But it didn't. We found a way. We never gave up.

Creative Corrections started as nothing more than an idea—a vision born from experience and necessity. But with determination, resourcefulness, and the support of a few good people, it became so much more.

And this? This was just the beginning.

Creative Corrections: How a Private Inspection Firm Rose to Tackle America's Prison Crisis

When Creative Corrections secured its first federal contract with the Office of the Federal Detention Trustee, it wasn't just a milestone; it was a launchpad. We understood the scope, the stakes, and the standards. And even without deep capital reserves, we delivered.

Relying on long-standing professional relationships and a reputation for integrity, we assembled a top-tier team willing to prioritize mission over money. That first audit wasn't just completed; it exceeded expectations. It established a precedent that continues to define us: do the work right, lead with integrity, and results will follow.

From day one, Creative Corrections has operated on the belief that rigorous, independent oversight is essential, not optional, in the correctional environment. Our commitment to transparency, data-driven assessments, and institutional accountability positioned us to respond to a national crisis with clarity and purpose.

The United States is home to the largest incarceration system in the world. With more than 1.9 million individuals housed in federal, state, and local jails and prisons, the American criminal justice system has grown into a sprawling and costly enterprise. Despite taxpayers spending over $80 billion annually to fund this system, the results remain alarmingly poor. Overcrowded facilities, rampant inefficiencies, minimal oversight, and high recidivism rates continue to plague American corrections.

It is in this environment that Creative Corrections emerged and found purpose. What sets Creative Corrections apart is its commitment to applying the rigor of accountability to one of the most opaque and bureaucratic sectors in the nation. While lawmakers and advocacy groups often pursue change through policy and litigation, Creative Corrections delivers results through real-time, independent inspection and evaluation. By focusing on operational efficiency, transparency, and sound correctional practices, the company established a critical role in modern correctional oversight.

We specialize in evaluating correctional operations against established, evidence-based correctional practices. Using highly experienced subject matter experts (SMEs) from the corrections field, we identify deficiencies, highlight areas of excellence, and support facilities in developing and implementing corrective action plans (CAPs).

Our company approaches correctional assessments not as a vendor, but as a professional evaluator. We are driven by a mission to promote safe, secure, and professionally operated correctional environments. Transparency and accountability should be the standard, not the exception. Our goal is to support operational excellence that is measurable, sustainable, and compliant with correctional best practices.

Among the most pressing issues we address is overcrowding and understaffing. Our inspections incorporate population management strategies, recognizing that overcrowding leads to increased violence, inadequate healthcare, staff burnout, and reduced program availability. Unlike other institutions, prisons cannot simply post a "No Vacancy" sign; therefore, the system must manage populations with operational strategies aligned with safety and care.

To support this need, Creative Corrections developed a comprehensive Assessment Tool. We offer frameworks that enable facilities to identify inefficiencies, mitigate liabilities, and enhance outcomes across operational, healthcare, mental health, education, and staffing domains. Our inspection protocol is a cornerstone of our work. It includes rigorous, on-site evaluations that assess compliance with security, health, and safety standards. These audits often lead to immediate improvements, including better sanitation, elimination of hazards, and enhanced access to medical care.

Staffing analyses complement these efforts. By identifying misallocated resources, we help facilities redirect funds to staff training, programming, and infrastructure. We also provide benchmarking tools to evaluate performance in areas like staffing efficiency, program availability, and grievance resolution.

Our clients include private companies, as well as local, state, and federal governments. Facilities use our services to meet mandates, comply with consent decrees, and improve internal operations. With over 3,000 jails and 1,800 prisons in the U.S., the potential for impact is significant.

Our results are measurable. Facilities report fewer use-of-force incidents, improved staff-inmate relations, and better planning capacity. Problems are addressed early, reducing legal exposure.

We have faced challenges, including maintaining independence, securing access, and clearly communicating our mission. But we meet these challenges with clarity and commitment. We do not profit from incarceration; we invest in safer, more effective correctional operations.

Chapter 7

A Transition

Creative Corrections has grown into a globally recognized leader in correctional facility consulting. Currently, the company conducts more than 200 detailed assessments of correctional institutions each year, providing strategic insight and operational recommendations to enhance facility performance, safety, and accountability. Our team has delivered professional services in over 30 countries across six continents, adapting to diverse legal systems, cultures, and correctional models. This global footprint reflects our flexibility, professionalism, and depth of expertise.

We are proud to have earned International Accreditation under the ISO 17020:2012, which has further solidified our reputation as a credible and trusted service provider in the corrections industry. This distinction not only validates our methodologies and ethical standards but also enables us to offer a wide array of specialized services —including training, auditing, and operational consulting—with recognized authority. We attribute our continued success to four foundational principles: Excellence, Integrity, Innovation, and Accountability. These values guide every aspect of our work and serve as the cornerstones of our corporate identity.

By Percy Pitzer

Beginning in 2022, our track record of excellence began to attract attention from several organizations expressing interest in acquiring Creative Corrections. Given my nearly 50 years of experience in the corrections field, I was open to the idea, provided it was the right fit. However, as I engaged in discussions with these prospective buyers, I quickly realized that most were primarily motivated by financial gain. Their intent appeared to be to acquire the company, repackage it, and resell it for a quick profit. This was fundamentally misaligned with our mission and vision. Our goal has always been to build a lasting institution—one that would continue to uphold our values and serve correctional systems with integrity for years to come. Selling to someone without that commitment would have been a disservice to our clients, our team, and the legacy we have built.

Then, in 2023, we received a pivotal phone call—one that would reshape the future of Creative Corrections. Stephen Spaulding reached out to express his interest in becoming a partner by acquiring a 49% ownership stake in the company. From our very first conversation, I sensed something different. Stephen wasn't a financier or an opportunist; he was a seasoned professional with a genuine passion for corrections. A retired Warden from the Federal Bureau of Prisons and a Rear Admiral with the United States Public Health Service, Stephen brought decades of hands-on experience, leadership, and operational insight to the table. His background aligned perfectly with our mission, and more importantly, his values mirrored my own.

Over the course of many in-depth conversations, it became clear to me that Stephen was the right person to help carry the company forward. He understood the importance of our work, respected the culture we had cultivated, and was genuinely interested in preserving and expanding the impact of Creative Corrections. Since officially becoming partners over a year ago, Stephen and I have worked closely to build on the company's strengths. Together, we have enhanced our service offerings, expanded our global presence, and solidified our reputation as a gold standard in correctional consulting.

Looking back, I have no doubt that I made the right decision. With Stephen as a partner, the legacy of Creative Corrections is in capable hands—and the future looks brighter than ever.

No immunity from life's challenges

Life is not always as smooth as you would like it to be. There are moments when the road seems straight and promising, and then, without warning, you find yourself navigating sharp turns you never anticipated. In the later part of 2003, we received a phone call that would shake the very foundation of our family. I was notified that my daughter Marsha had become addicted to drugs and alcohol. The words hit me like a freight train. We were aware she had been having "issues"—occasional mood swings, money troubles, and instability in her relationships—but like so many other families, we never realized the depth or gravity of what was really happening. We hoped it was just a rough patch. We rationalized, minimized, and sometimes even ignored the warning signs, convincing ourselves that she would pull through it on her own.

Marsha was living in Beaumont, Texas, with her young daughter, Ashley. The distance between us suddenly felt insurmountable. Both Sue and I were at a loss—what do we do, and how do we handle this devastating curveball? How do you respond when the child you once held in your arms is now a parent herself, spiraling into addiction and dragging an innocent child into the chaos with her?

Sue, always more in charge when it came to matters of the heart, didn't hesitate. The very next day, she boarded a plane to Texas. Her intuition told her this was not something we could wait on. When she arrived, she met with Marsha and a representative from the Department of Children Services. The conversation was tense, layered with emotion and uncertainty. After a lengthy discussion, they concluded that while Marsha was struggling, the situation wasn't quite as dire as originally reported. There was, at least on the surface, a flicker of hope. Sue returned to Las Vegas, relieved, but she carried an uneasiness in her gut that never truly went away.

That uneasy feeling proved to be justified. Just a couple of months later, the situation took a sharp and frightening turn for the worse. We learned that Marsha's condition had deteriorated significantly. Her addiction had deepened, and while we were terrified for her well-being, our greater concern was for little Ashley. She was far too young to fend for herself, emotionally or physically. Every night, we found ourselves lying awake, wondering what was happening in that household, questioning how long we could stand by before stepping in more forcefully. It was then that we made one of the hardest decisions of our lives—we left everything behind and relocated back to Beaumont.

Over the next few years, we hoped—desperately—that our physical presence might make a difference. That somehow, just being there would snap Marsha out of her addiction. But nothing we did seemed to help. We cried, we pleaded, we reasoned, we threatened. We tried to love her back to sobriety, to guilt her into recovery, to finance her way out of addiction. But none of it worked. It became painfully clear that even our family, with all our resources, values, and intentions, was not immune to the cruel grip of addiction. Over time, Marsha enrolled in nine different treatment centers. Nine. That included a premier, world-renowned program in Thailand, which we had hoped would be a turning point. But like the others, it failed to bring lasting change.

It was a financial strain, of course, but thanks to the prosperity of our business, we were able to afford these options. Still, with every failed program, it felt like we were tossing money into a well with no bottom. We came to a hard but necessary realization—if Marsha was ever going to recover, it wouldn't be because of us. It wouldn't be because of any program, lecture, or threat. It would only happen if *she* made the decision to fight for her life, to believe that her life was worth saving.

Meanwhile, the turmoil within our family only grew. Ashley, who had now entered her teenage years, faced her own challenges. She became pregnant at 16. Already struggling in school and showing signs of withdrawal, her pregnancy pushed us to the brink emotionally. We felt like we were spiraling. Questions plagued us constantly: Had we failed her? Could we really help anyone at this point? Were we losing not just our daughter, but our granddaughter as well?

And yet, amidst the chaos, glimmers of hope appeared. One of those glimmers came in the form of a compassionate assistant principal—someone who refused to let Ashley fall through the cracks. This educator became a guiding force for her. After giving birth to her daughter, Ashley returned to school with renewed determination. Slowly but surely, she climbed her way back. Not only did she finish high school, but she eventually earned a master's degree in business. That journey, filled with setbacks and small triumphs, reminded us that redemption is possible, even when the odds seem insurmountable.

As for Marsha, her struggle continued. She was arrested for possession of a controlled substance and placed on probation. Even then, she could not break free from the cycle of use. Desperate and out of options, I made one of the most gut-wrenching phone calls of my life. I contacted her probation officer and confessed that she was still using drugs. He elevated her to a higher level of supervision, but the behavior persisted. Eventually, I called again, and this time I didn't mince words. I told him that if he didn't intervene—if he didn't get her off the streets—I would go straight to the judge myself. It was an act of desperation, but also of love. The kind of love that forces you to make the hardest choices, not for yourself, but for someone else's survival.

Marsha was arrested again and placed in a court-ordered, nine-month rehabilitation program. She relapsed afterward, as many do, but there was a significant shift. For the next several years, she managed to remain substance-free. We clung to that progress. But the reality of addiction is that it's a lifelong battle. You're never entirely out of the woods. Even today, we live with the uncertainty of not knowing if or when the darkness might creep back in.

Throughout this journey, Sue and I often asked ourselves where we went wrong. What could we have done differently? In our search for answers, we reflected on Marsha's childhood and the many disruptions she experienced due to my career. One moment stood out sharply in our memory. When she was nine years old, and we were living in New York, she came home from school in tears. She told us the other kids were calling her a "Chinese creep." That phrase hit us like a punch to the stomach. Sue is of Asian descent, but in our home, Marsha was simply our daughter—loved, cherished, and whole. We never imagined others would see her differently.

Marsha's pain was palpable. That incident opened our eyes to a silent burden she had been carrying—one we had overlooked. It seemed she had learned early on that acceptance often came at the cost of suppressing her identity and striving to please others. We began to wonder how many other slurs or insults she had endured that we never knew about. Children don't always share everything, and sometimes their silence speaks volumes.

I scheduled a meeting with her teacher, hoping for empathy. Instead, I was told, rather matter-of-factly, "Marsha needs to learn how to stand up for herself." I was stunned. "At nine years old?" I asked. The teacher shrugged. Dissatisfied, I went to the principal, only to encounter something worse. "It must be her time of the month," he said with a dismissive laugh. His cruelty was staggering. I left that office fuming, feeling helpless and furious. I couldn't believe how deeply rooted prejudice and indifference still were, especially in places meant to nurture children.

The experience reminded me of the timeless lyrics from *South Pacific*: "You've got to be carefully taught." The song's message—that hatred and bias are learned—still rings tragically true today.

So why share all of this, especially while recounting the early stages of building our business? Because no one is immune to life's challenges—not me, not you, not even those who appear to have it all together. We can dress our wounds in success and smile through the pain, but that doesn't mean the pain isn't there. What good does it do to hide it?

Timing is a part of the unfoldment of every story. And mine—both personal and professional—is no exception. As a retired prison warden, I now use my experiences, both painful and powerful, to educate others. My focus is on improving quality and expanding opportunity within the correctional field. Life doesn't always go as planned. But through hardship, heartbreak, and healing, we can discover a deeper purpose. We can use our scars not as signs of defeat, but as evidence of survival—and, if we're fortunate, of growth.

Recognizing another need

What began as a professional concern evolved into something far deeper—a moral and economic imperative. We took a step back and looked at the broader picture, and the statistics were staggering. More than five million children in the United States have had a parent incarcerated at some point in their lives. These children are six times more likely to end up in prison themselves. They are significantly more likely to drop out of school, live in poverty, suffer from emotional trauma, and face barriers to employment and stability. Incarceration in America isn't just institutional—it's generational.

In 2012 Sue and I founded the Pitzer Family Education Foundation with a clear and personal goal: to provide scholarships to children of incarcerated parents. This initiative was to target a broader truth that many of the individuals housed in the facilities we inspected came from communities plagued by systemic barriers long before incarceration became a reality.

Again and again, we encountered the same story—generational cycles of disadvantage, disrupted families, and children placed at risk through no fault of their own. It became clear that while we could help correctional facilities operate more safely and effectively, the long-term solution also required proactive investment in the lives of those most vulnerable to the ripple effects of incarceration.

The Pitzer Family Education Foundation was created to meet that need. Through scholarships, mentorship, and community partnerships, the Foundation provides resources that give children of incarcerated parents a chance to pursue a different path, one shaped by education, not incarceration.

This effort is not about charity. It is about equity. It is about equipping the next generation with tools to break cycles that data shows are otherwise all too predictable. Just as Creative Corrections champions operational excellence within correctional institutions, the Foundation works to create pathways of hope and possibility outside of them.

But vision alone doesn't build a foundation. It takes people—dedicated, passionate, skilled individuals—to turn that vision into a reality. I consider myself profoundly fortunate to have found such people in Anthony Haynes, my daughter Marsha Pitzer, and Mary Williams.

Anthony Haynes joined the foundation as our Executive Director in January 2014. With over 30 years of experience in law enforcement and corrections, including distinguished service in the United States Air Force and leadership roles in the Federal Bureau of Prisons, Anthony brought unmatched credibility and insight to our team. His career took him from patrolling military bases during Operation Desert Storm to overseeing complex correctional institutions as a member of the Senior Executive Service. He had seen the system from every angle.

But Anthony's value to our foundation extended far beyond his résumé. What made him truly indispensable was his heart—his unwavering belief in second chances, his empathy for families torn apart by incarceration, and his ability to inspire others to act. Under his leadership, the Pitzer Family Education Foundation didn't just grow—it was transformed. Anthony spearheaded the formation of partnerships with more than fourteen state departments of corrections. He also initiated groundbreaking programs that encouraged incarcerated parents to take ownership of their children's futures. Through these efforts, over $250,000 in donations were raised directly from incarcerated individuals—men and women who, despite their circumstances, chose to invest in their children's education. That message—that even from within prison walls, redemption can take the form of generational change—became a central pillar of our work. And Anthony has been, and remains, its most powerful voice.

While Anthony was expanding our presence nationwide, my daughter Marsha anchored our efforts at home. As Program Administrator, she serves as the operational backbone of the foundation. Marsha ensures that every scholarship application is handled with care and confidentiality. Every student file is secure, every deadline met, every outreach campaign executed with precision. But her impact goes far beyond logistics. Marsha is the face of the foundation in our communities. Whether she's coordinating with the Associated Builders and Contractors Training Academy in Nederland, Texas, engaging with families at local job fairs, or representing the foundation at state conferences, Marsha is constantly working to connect underserved youth with new opportunities.

Her tireless efforts to build and maintain relationships with local organizations, educators, and donors have not only increased the visibility of our mission but also secured the funding necessary to keep scholarships flowing. Marsha understands that behind every application is a story—a child dreaming of a future, a family hoping for a fresh start. She treats those stories with the respect and dedication they deserve.

Supporting all of this with quiet consistency and steadfast dependability is Mary Williams, our Administrative Assistant. Mary's role may be behind the scenes, but her contributions are vital. She manages our schedules, facilitates communication between departments, prepares reports, and ensures that the day-to-day operations of the foundation run smoothly and efficiently. Her collaboration with Marsha forms the bedrock of our administrative processes. During times of rapid growth or unexpected challenges, Mary is the one who brings calm, order, and clarity. Her attention to detail ensures that nothing falls through the cracks—and her commitment to excellence keeps our entire team moving forward.

Together, Anthony, Marsha, and Mary have taken the Pitzer Family Education Foundation from an idea to a movement. They have brought our mission into prisons, classrooms, courtrooms, homes, and policy discussions. Through their combined efforts, they have instilled hope in children who once felt forgotten, empowered incarcerated parents to reclaim a role in their children's futures, and strengthened the credibility and reach of our organization.

As I reflect on this journey, I'm overwhelmed with gratitude. The progress we've made is not the result of one person's effort—it's the collective achievement of a team united by compassion, justice, and an unshakable belief in the power of education. Because of Anthony's leadership, Marsha's determination, and Mary's reliability, we continue to grow stronger and more resilient each day. And because of them, we remain firmly committed to changing lives—one child, one family, one future at a time.

And with every step forward, we remain guided by the belief that education is not just a tool—it is a lifeline. One that can reach across generations, rewrite stories, and illuminate paths once shrouded in darkness.

The Economic Argument for Prevention Over Punishment

The economic case for this transition is undeniable. The United States spends over $80 billion annually on corrections, according to the Prison Policy Initiative. When the full range of indirect costs—such as lost wages, decreased economic output, and added social services—are considered, the Brennan Center for Justice estimates that number balloons to more than $182 billion year.

On a per-person basis, the financial burden is also staggering. A 2021 report from Pew Charitable Trusts estimated the average cost to incarcerate one person in state prison at approximately $39,158 per year. In states with higher costs, that figure can exceed $60,000. Meanwhile, the National Center for Education Statistics reports that the average annual cost of educating a public-school student is about $13,185.

That contrast illustrates a basic truth: we are paying three to five times more to incarcerate people than we would to educate them. And the disparity compounds over time. A person incarcerated for 20 years at $40,000 per year will cost taxpayers $800,000. That same sum could fund over a dozen full four-year college scholarships or support sixty years of K–12 education for one student.

More importantly, incarceration carries a host of long-term public costs. Formerly incarcerated individuals often face lifelong barriers to employment, housing, and healthcare. They are more likely to require public assistance and are significantly more likely to reoffend. According to the Bureau of Justice Statistics, roughly 68% of released prisoners are rearrested within three years; 77% within five years.

We came to understand that without early intervention—especially for the children of incarcerated individuals—the criminal justice system becomes a cycle that is not only morally troubling, but economically unsustainable.

The Risks Facing Children of Incarcerated Parents

Children of incarcerated parents represent one of the most at-risk populations in the United States. More than 5 million children have had a parent incarcerated at some point, according to the Annie E. Casey Foundation. These children are not only more likely to live in poverty, but also more likely to face emotional trauma, housing instability, and educational disruption.

Research consistently shows that children with incarcerated parents are more likely to:

- Struggle academically
- Experience behavioral issues
- Drop out of school
- Encounter the juvenile justice system
- Suffer from depression or anxiety
- Live in unstable or overcrowded households

Perhaps most alarmingly, they are significantly more likely to be incarcerated themselves. A study from the Urban Institute found that children of incarcerated parents are six times more likely to end up in prison than their peers. This trend is not coincidental—it reflects a systemic failure to intervene at a crucial stage in the life cycle of justice involvement.

This is why our work had to change. The scale of the problem demanded more than better prisons. It required a new front line of defense: education.

The Preventive Power of Education

Education is one of the most effective deterrents to future incarceration. It is also one of the strongest predictors of lifetime success. According to the U.S. Bureau of Labor Statistics, individuals without a high school diploma had a 2023 unemployment rate of 5.4% and a median weekly income of $682. Those with a bachelor's degree had an unemployment rate of just 2.2% and earned $1,432 per week—more than double.

The lifetime earnings gap between someone with only a high school diploma and someone with a four-year degree exceeds $1 million. And that economic benefit translates to stronger communities, lower crime rates, and greater overall stability.

The RAND Corporation found that inmates who participated in

education programs while incarcerated were 43% less likely to return to prison. That statistic powerfully illustrates education's impact—even when it's delivered late in life. But it also raises a critical question: *What if that education came sooner?*

Investing in the education of at-risk youth, particularly those with incarcerated parents, is not merely compassionate—it is cost-effective. According to the Washington State Institute for Public Policy, every dollar spent on high-quality early education returns $7 to $12 in long-term benefits. That includes reduced criminal activity, improved health outcomes, and increased earnings.

The Brookings Institution has similarly found that targeted interventions—such as after-school programs, family counseling, and academic tutoring—significantly reduce crime and long-term justice involvement. These programs often cost a fraction of what incarceration does and offer measurable long-term returns.

A Strategic Shift Toward Long-Term Change

Our decision to add a nonprofit education mission was not just a shift in operations. It was a complete reorientation toward long-term impact. Both organizations serve a critical purpose.

We still wanted to be the ones ensuring that prison systems ran smoothly—but we also wanted to help reduce the number of people entering those systems in the first place. That required a systemic approach: partnering with schools, working with communities, supporting families, and reaching children early enough to make a difference.

Our refined mission focuses on identifying and supporting children of incarcerated parents through:

- Academic support and tutoring
- Mentorship and life-skills development
- Family engagement initiatives
- Trauma-informed mental health services

- After-school and summer enrichment programs
- Scholarships and postsecondary preparation

We are also committed to raising public awareness about the economic and social benefits of early intervention. By building partnerships with local education agencies, correctional institutions, and nonprofit organizations, we are creating a network of support that recognizes and responds to the unique challenges these children face.

Why This Matters Now

The intergenerational cycle of incarceration is not an abstract concept. It is a reality experienced in thousands of communities across the country. It is sustained by systemic inequality, chronic underinvestment in public education, and the failure to support families in crisis.

Breaking that cycle requires a different kind of investment—one rooted not in punishment, but in prevention.

Policymakers can and should act. Among the most effective steps:

- Identify and support affected children within schools and social service systems.
- Create partnerships between schools, correctional systems, and nonprofits.
- Fund early childhood education in communities with high incarceration rates.
- Facilitate parent engagement from within prisons to maintain family bonds.
- Support after-school and enrichment programs that keep children safe and engaged.
- Establish scholarship funds dedicated to children of incarcerated parents.

These investments are modest compared to the long-term cost of incarceration. And they carry with them the potential not only to change individual lives, but to fundamentally alter the future of families and communities.

We expanded beyond Creative Corrections not because we lost faith in reform—but because we gained clarity about prevention. After years inside the system, we saw the patterns too clearly to ignore: Incarceration is often the result of early, unmet needs. By meeting those needs—particularly in the lives of children whose parents are already incarcerated—we can intervene in the most meaningful way.

The truth is simple and supported by data: It is cheaper to educate the child of an inmate than to incarcerate that child as an adult.

But beyond cost, it is better. It is just. It is hopeful.

We believe that every child—regardless of their parents' past—deserves the opportunity to build a future that is not defined by incarceration, but by potential.

This is our new mission. And we believe it's the most important work we've ever done.

How inmates helped fund a better future

Most people wouldn't think to ask inmates to donate to a college scholarship fund. But I've never been one to accept limitations—especially when it comes to breaking the cycle of incarceration.

I learned early on that incarcerated people, though often overlooked, can be powerful agents of change. Years ago, while working at a prison in El Paso, a local police officer was killed in the line of duty. The department and a handful of nonprofits were scrambling to raise money to buy bulletproof vests for officers still on duty. I had an idea that most would have dismissed outright: let's ask the inmates to donate.

The initial reaction? Just what you'd expect—both from the staff and from the inmates. "You must be crazy," they said. The inmates themselves had a few more... colorful words. But I spoke to them plainly. I said, "If your family is in danger—if your wife, your mother, your kids have to call for help—do you trust the Black Gangster Disciples or the Aryan Brotherhood to show up and protect them? Or do you want someone wearing a vest who's trained to respond and help?" That hit home. One of them looked at me and said, "Well, when you put it that way..."

That moment stuck with me. It proved something important: inmates will do whatever you ask them to do—if it makes sense. They're the products of the prison system, yes, but that also means they can be part of the solution.

Years later, when we founded the Pitzer Family Education Foundation, I knew we had to involve them again—this time, to help keep their own kids from ending up in the same place. We created a college scholarship fund for children of incarcerated parents. The mission was simple but powerful: invest in education over incarceration. Help these kids build a future that doesn't involve orange jumpsuits or metal bars.

And we went back to the same people society had written off— the inmates themselves. Again, some folks thought I was crazy. But I didn't see inmates—I saw fathers, mothers, uncles, aunts. I saw people who, given the chance, would do right by their kids. And they did.

To date, incarcerated individuals from 14 state departments of corrections have donated over $250,000 to the foundation. That money has helped us provide more than 200 scholarships for children of incarcerated parents to attend college or trade school. But the support doesn't stop there. Our team works together with each student to navigate the financial aid process, ensuring that every scholarship dollar stretches as far as possible. We want them to succeed—not just academically, but as whole people.

The ripple effect doesn't stop with the kids. We also provide educational opportunities to returning citizens and at-risk young adults in communities across Southeast Texas. Through partnerships with Lamar State College Port Arthur and the Associated Builders and Contractors Training Academy in Nederland, Texas, we help individuals learn a trade, earn a degree, and step into careers that break the generational cycle of incarceration.

This work has proven a simple truth: redemption doesn't come from the outside in. It comes from within. And sometimes, the people who seem furthest from the solution turn out to be the ones most committed to making change happen.

Chapter 8

Policy Matters: Understanding the Foundations of Recidivism Reform

Recidivism remains one of the most persistent challenges in the American criminal justice system. The repeated incarceration of individuals after their release from prison isn't simply a symptom of personal failure or moral weakness; it is often the consequence of systemic barriers, insufficient support, and shortsighted policies. Politicians play a pivotal role in either perpetuating these cycles or dismantling them through thoughtful, evidence-based reform. Addressing recidivism is about more than reducing crime statistics—it's about rebuilding communities, empowering individuals, and ensuring public safety through sustainable change.

Several core policies consistently emerge as effective tools in combating recidivism. Each of these must be understood not as isolated measures but as interconnected strategies that support successful reentry and long-term societal reintegration.

1. "Ban the Box" Legislation

Employment is one of the strongest predictors of post-incarceration success. Yet many individuals face immediate discrimination when applying for jobs due to criminal history checkboxes on applications. "Ban the Box" legislation addresses this by delaying inquiries into criminal records until later in the hiring process, giving applicants a chance to demonstrate their qualifications first. Studies have shown that when individuals are allowed to explain their histories during interviews rather than being screened out at the application stage, their chances of securing employment increase substantially. Political support for such policies signals a commitment to restorative justice and economic inclusion.

2. Record Expungement and Sealing

Many individuals continue to carry the weight of their criminal records long after they have served their time. These records can prevent access to housing, employment, education, and even voting rights in some jurisdictions. Policies that allow for the expungement or sealing of records—especially for non-violent offenses or after a designated period of good conduct—offer people a genuine opportunity to move on. Automatic expungement measures, which remove the burden from individuals to navigate complex legal processes, have been particularly impactful. Politicians who champion these efforts are often those willing to address the long-term consequences of over-criminalization.

3. Comprehensive Reentry Support

Reentry does not begin the day someone walks out of prison—it begins months, sometimes years, earlier. Effective policies recognize this and allocate funding for transitional planning that includes housing assistance, job training, access to healthcare, and mental health and substance abuse treatment. Without these resources, formerly incarcerated individuals are left to navigate complex societal systems on their own, increasing the likelihood of reoffending. Legislative leaders must push for the expansion and funding of such programs not as charity, but as smart public policy.

4. Education and Job Training in Correctional Facilities

In-prison educational programs—from GED preparation and vocational training to associate and bachelor's degrees—are among the most reliable predictors of reduced recidivism. Individuals who engage in educational activities while incarcerated are significantly less likely to return to prison. Moreover, vocational training aligned with market demands can enable individuals to reenter the workforce with real, competitive skills. Political leadership is essential in securing funding for such programs and resisting efforts to cut educational services from correctional budgets.

5. Parole and Probation Reform

Probation and parole systems, originally designed as alternatives to incarceration, have increasingly become traps for re-incarceration due to technical violations such as missing meetings or failing drug tests. These are not new criminal acts, yet they often result in imprisonment. Reimagining supervision as a supportive, rather than punitive, mechanism involves training officers to act as case managers and ensuring that resources—rather than punishment—are used to address the underlying causes of noncompliance. Legislators must push for reforms that reduce reincarceration for technical violations and align supervision with public health and rehabilitation goals.

Lessons from States That Have Led the Way

The most successful reforms have emerged from a mix of bipartisan commitment, community advocacy, and data-driven strategies. Several states offer instructive examples:

Texas: In the mid-2000s, Texas faced a prison overcrowding crisis. Instead of investing in more prisons, lawmakers—through bipartisan cooperation—redirected funds toward mental health treatment, drug courts, and reentry programs. As a result, the state closed multiple prisons, saved billions of dollars, and saw a significant decline in its recidivism and crime rates. The Texas model demonstrated that smart investment in community-based alternatives could yield both economic and public safety dividends.

Georgia: Georgia took an aggressive approach to criminal justice reform by creating a Criminal Justice Reform Council tasked with analyzing data and recommending evidence-based changes. The state reduced mandatory minimums for nonviolent offenses, expanded access to specialty courts, and created a state-level agency dedicated to reentry. These coordinated efforts have resulted in a notable drop in recidivism rates and a growing consensus that thoughtful reform pays off.

Oregon: Long recognized for its progressive approach, Oregon has integrated criminal justice with public health. Its use of risk assessments and individualized supervision plans ensures that resources go where they are most needed. Community-based corrections, investment in addiction treatment, and a strong emphasis on family reunification have allowed Oregon to maintain one of the lowest recidivism rates in the country. These outcomes were achieved through sustained political commitment and a culture of continuous evaluation and improvement.

Red Flags in Political Rhetoric

Despite these successes, many political leaders still default to outdated narratives around crime and punishment. Voters and advocates should be wary of rhetoric that appeals to fear rather than facts.

- Overemphasis on "tough on crime" language often signals a reluctance to embrace rehabilitative strategies. Such framing prioritizes punishment over transformation and typically results in policies that exacerbate recidivism.
- Vague or symbolic commitments to "supporting second chances" without actionable policy details should raise concern. Statements unaccompanied by legislative proposals or budgetary commitments are more likely to be political theater than genuine reform.
- Inconsistent legislative behavior is another warning sign. Politicians who express support for criminal justice reform but oppose funding for reentry programs, housing

initiatives, or mental health services are not aligning their words with action.

- Fear-based appeals that use isolated incidents of reoffending to advocate against broader reforms distort the evidence and stigmatize formerly incarcerated individuals.

Holding Elected Officials Accountable: Interrogating the Platform

Evaluating a candidate's position on criminal justice reform requires looking beyond campaign slogans. Serious reformers typically outline clear proposals in their platforms. These may include:

- Specific investments in reentry services, with budgetary figures
- Detailed positions on record expungement and sealing laws
- Strategies to provide in-prison education and post-release employment assistance
- Plans to overhaul parole and probation systems
- Support for ending civil penalties such as voting disenfranchisement

When candidates avoid these specifics or defer to vague language, it is often an indication that reform is not a priority.

Questions That Demand Accountability

Active civic engagement is essential. Town halls, debates, and public forums offer rare opportunities to directly question those seeking or holding office. Some questions that can reveal a politician's commitment to reform include:

- "What specific policies will you support to ensure that reentry services are adequately funded and accessible to all returning citizens?"
- "Would you support automatic expungement of criminal records for non-violent offenses, and how would you implement such a policy?"
- "How will your office ensure incarcerated individuals have access to education and job training programs?"
- "Do you support reforms to probation and parole that reduce re-incarceration for technical violations?"
- "Can you provide examples of legislation you have introduced or supported that directly addresses recidivism?"

These questions press candidates to go beyond platitudes and speak to measurable outcomes.

What Makes a Truly Reform-Minded Leader?

To determine whether a politician is truly committed to reform, consider the following:

- Legislative history: Have they consistently supported bills that expand access to services for formerly incarcerated individuals?
- Budgetary decisions: Do they prioritize funding for programs that support successful reentry?
- Engagement with affected communities: Do they meet regularly with advocacy groups and individuals impacted by the system?
- Transparency and data use: Do they advocate for data collection, public reporting, and performance measurement in justice programs?

- Bipartisanship: Are they willing to work across ideological lines to support sustainable reforms?

From the Inside Out: The Role of Civic Engagement in Reintegration

For individuals reentering society, civic engagement can be a transformative tool. Participation in democratic processes—particularly voting—can help restore a sense of agency and belonging. Research shows that individuals who vote and engage with their communities after incarceration are significantly less likely to reoffend. This is not merely symbolic. It represents a realignment of identity, from outsider to contributor.

Unfortunately, many states continue to bar individuals with felony convictions from voting, either permanently or through opaque restoration processes. Eliminating these barriers and ensuring automatic restoration of voting rights post-release is an essential step toward reinforcing the idea that rehabilitation is possible and supported.

Advocacy and Systemic Change

Formerly incarcerated individuals are uniquely positioned to inform criminal justice reform. Their firsthand experiences provide valuable insight into the failures and successes of the system. Policy advocacy led by affected individuals is among the most powerful forces for change. These individuals not only humanize the issue but also bring credibility and urgency to the discussion.

Political leaders must do more than listen to these voices—they must make space for them in decision-making processes. Task forces, advisory councils, and legislative hearings should include representation from those with lived experience. Funding community-based organizations that focus on reentry and advocacy can amplify these efforts and create a feedback loop that continually improves policy outcomes.

The fight against recidivism is a fight for justice, safety, and human dignity. It requires policies that see people as capable of change, systems that prioritize support over punishment, and political leadership grounded in data and compassion. The evidence is over-whelming: when we invest in reentry, reform supervision, erase unnecessary barriers, and empower individuals through civic engage-ment, we reduce recidivism and strengthen society.

Politicians have the tools to drive this change. Voters have the responsibility to demand it. Through transparency, accountability, and sustained advocacy, the cycle of incarceration can be broken—not just for individuals, but for entire communities.

Chapter 9

Second Chance Hiring: The Talent Pipeline We're Ignoring

I n an era marked by persistent labor shortages, rising inflation, and a rapidly aging workforce, American businesses are facing mounting challenges in filling essential roles across virtually every sector. From fast food restaurants that can't staff enough cooks to construction firms desperate for skilled tradespeople, the labor crisis is no longer a looming threat—it's a daily operational obstacle. According to the U.S. Chamber of Commerce, there are consistently more job openings than unemployed individuals to fill them. While automation, offshoring, and gig work have addressed some of the pressure points, these strategies are neither sustainable nor scalable for every industry. The long-term solution may lie in an overlooked, misunderstood, and significantly underutilized workforce: returning citizens—individuals reentering society after incarceration.

Approximately 600,000 people are released from state and federal prisons each year in the United States. This number does not account for the millions more cycling through local jails. Despite being eager to work and contribute to society, formerly incarcerated individuals face an unemployment rate of over 27%, according to the Prison Policy Initiative. This is higher than the national average during the Great Depression. The primary barriers include criminal background checks, employer stigma, and lack of access to workforce development services. While some employers cite concerns over reliability, security, and liability, emerging evidence demonstrates that many of these fears are based more on perception than reality.

Companies that have embraced second-chance hiring report overwhelmingly positive outcomes. At Butterball Farms in Michigan, returning citizens make up a significant share of the workforce. CEO Mark Peters has publicly credited these employees with lower turnover rates and a higher degree of company loyalty than other workers. The firm's inclusive culture has not only improved employee morale but also enhanced overall productivity. Similarly, Dave's Killer Bread—a bakery founded by Dave Dahl, a formerly incarcerated entrepreneur—has woven second-chance employment into its corporate DNA. Their hiring practices have contributed to a resilient workforce that reflects a culture of redemption and mutual respect.

More broadly, companies like JPMorgan Chase, Total Wine & More, and Koch Industries have launched comprehensive second-chance initiatives. These efforts include removing blanket bans on criminal records, offering targeted training, and providing access to support services. Their success signals a shifting tide in corporate America, where second-chance hiring is no longer seen as a risky experiment but a viable, competitive strategy.

A 2017 study by researchers at Harvard University and the University of Massachusetts Amherst found that workers with criminal records often stay with their employers longer than those without. This loyalty results in significant savings on recruitment and training, areas that traditionally drain corporate budgets. High turnover has long plagued industries such as hospitality, manufacturing, and retail. If returning citizens can fill these roles with greater dedication and staying power, then businesses stand to gain both operational stability and cost-efficiency.

Nevertheless, concerns over insurance, workplace safety, and legal liability remain common. Employers worry about the risk of negligent hiring lawsuits or workplace incidents. However, these risks can be effectively managed. Many states participate in the Federal Bonding Program, which provides no-cost fidelity bonds to employers as a form of insurance against employee dishonesty or theft. These bonds serve as a safety net, reducing perceived financial risk. Additionally, companies can establish clear internal policies and procedures aligned with the Equal Employment Opportunity Commission's (EEOC) guidelines to minimize legal exposure. Risk management should be approached not as a barrier, but as a manageable component of a comprehensive hiring strategy.

Building a Second-Chance Hiring Program

Building a second-chance hiring initiative involves more than a revised application form or a single hiring event. It requires a strategic, intentional commitment across multiple levels of the organization. Successful programs integrate second-chance hiring into the company's HR framework, align with broader business objectives, and provide the necessary support to ensure long-term retention and success.

The foundational step is to examine and update existing hiring policies. Many companies still use outdated screening criteria that automatically disqualify applicants with criminal records. These blanket bans, whether explicit or embedded in background check protocols, are not only discriminatory but potentially illegal under EEOC guidelines. The EEOC recommends a more nuanced approach—conducting individualized assessments that consider the nature of the offense, how much time has passed since the conviction, and whether the offense is relevant to the job being applied for. Removing the box that asks about criminal history on initial applications—a practice known as "ban the box"—can help reduce unconscious bias and ensure that candidates are evaluated on their qualifications first.

Once policies are revised, HR teams and hiring managers must be trained to implement them effectively. This training should go beyond compliance. It should include education on the social and economic costs of mass incarceration, the challenges of reentry, and the business case for second-chance hiring. Role-playing exercises, bias training, and case studies can help HR professionals develop the skills and empathy needed to assess candidates fairly. This process also builds internal confidence, increasing the likelihood that second-chance hiring becomes institutionalized rather than dependent on a single champion within the company.

However, hiring is just the beginning. Returning citizens often face a complex web of reentry challenges. These may include lack of housing, limited access to transportation, untreated mental health conditions, and strained family relationships. Without support, even the most promising employee can struggle to succeed. Employers should consider offering or facilitating wraparound services that address these challenges. This might include partnering with organizations that provide housing support, addiction counseling, legal assistance, or financial literacy training. Companies can also implement peer mentorship programs where experienced employees guide new hires through the transition.

At Greyston Bakery in New York, the company's "Open Hiring" model eliminates interviews and background checks altogether. Anyone who wants a job puts their name on a list and is hired when a position becomes available. Greyston complements this radical approach with robust support services that help employees navigate personal and professional challenges. This model has not only stabilized the company's workforce but also attracted national attention as a pioneering example of inclusive employment.

Partnerships are essential to scaling second-chance hiring efforts. Nonprofits such as the Center for Employment Opportunities, Defy Ventures, and the Safer Foundation specialize in preparing justice-impacted individuals for the workforce. These organizations offer job readiness training, mock interviews, resume building, and case management. Workforce development boards and local chambers of commerce can also provide access to funding, tax incentives, and strategic planning resources.

In some cases, businesses are going directly to the source by forming partnerships with correctional facilities. The Last Mile, for instance, offers incarcerated individuals intensive training in software development. Employers who collaborate with such programs can build talent pipelines by offering apprenticeships, internships, or conditional job offers contingent on release. These initiatives ensure that individuals leave prison with not just hope but marketable skills and a direct connection to gainful employment.

Measuring Success and Impact

No business initiative is complete without a framework for measuring success. Second-chance hiring should be evaluated through a lens of return on investment, productivity, and cultural impact. Employers can track retention rates, absenteeism, promotion frequency, and employee engagement scores to assess how returning citizens contribute to the workforce compared to traditional hires.

Companies like Total Wine & More have used data to validate the success of their second-chance efforts. By analyzing employee performance and turnover metrics, they found that justice-impacted employees performed on par with or better than their peers. These results provided the internal justification needed to expand the program and strengthen their partnership with reentry organizations.

Cost savings from reduced turnover and rehiring expenses can also be quantified. According to the Society for Human Resource Management (SHRM), the average cost-per-hire is over \$4,000. High employee churn magnifies these costs. If second-chance employees stay longer and exhibit high levels of engagement, the financial benefits can quickly outweigh initial implementation costs.

Integrating second-chance hiring into workforce strategies is an impactful approach. The criminal justice system disproportionately impacts certain communities, particularly Black and Hispanic men.

By focusing on hiring justice-impacted individuals, companies demonstrate a broader commitment to fairness and social responsibility. Key measures could include the number of returning citizens employed, their advancement within the company, and their presence in leadership development programs.

The reputational value of second-chance hiring should not be underestimated. In today's values-driven marketplace, consumers and employees are increasingly making decisions based on a company's social responsibility record. Businesses that promote second-chance hiring often find themselves the subject of positive media coverage, community goodwill, and increased employee loyalty. This reputational capital can be especially valuable in competitive industries where brand differentiation is key.

Culturally, second-chance hiring can transform a workplace. Employees feel proud to work for a company that believes in second chances. Managers develop new skills in coaching and mentorship. Teams become more diverse—not just in demographics but in lived experience. These changes foster innovation, resilience, and a shared sense of purpose. As returning citizens integrate successfully, they become some of the company's strongest advocates and mentors for others.

Moreover, the societal impact is profound. Stable employment is one of the most significant predictors of successful reentry. The Brookings Institution has found that individuals who secure employment shortly after release are significantly less likely to return to prison. Reducing recidivism has broad implications: lower incarceration costs, fewer crime victims, stronger families, and healthier communities. Employers who participate in this ecosystem aren't just filling jobs—they're helping to rewrite life stories.

For policymakers, the economic case is equally compelling. The United States spends over $80 billion annually on incarceration. Redirecting even a fraction of that cost toward workforce development and employer incentives can yield massive returns in productivity and public safety. Businesses that lead in second-chance hiring can influence public policy, encourage legislative support, and shape a more inclusive economy.

Ultimately, addressing recidivism through employment is a rare win-win-win: for businesses, for individuals, and for society. Companies that embrace second-chance hiring gain access to a resilient labor pool, reduce turnover, and enhance their public image. Returning citizens find dignity, purpose, and stability. And communities become safer and more economically vibrant. The evidence is clear, the tools are available, and the need is urgent. It's time to stop ignoring this talent pipeline and start building the inclusive workforce of the future—one second chance at a time.

Chapter 10

No Place to Go

When a person walks out of prison, they often carry nothing more than the clothes on their back and a few dollars in their pocket. But the most burdensome thing they carry is invisible: a stigma that can close nearly every door that society claims to offer. For the more than 600,000 individuals released from state and federal prisons each year in the United States, the challenge of reentry is immediate and brutal. Chief among their obstacles is housing. Without a stable place to live, everything else—employment, healthcare, sobriety, and family reunification—becomes infinitely harder.

For many returning citizens, the transition begins with hope and optimism. After years behind bars, they look forward to rejoining families, rebuilding careers, and contributing to their communities. But that hope often encounters a harsh reality: few employers will hire them, fewer landlords will rent to them, and even fewer systems are designed to support them. The phrase "paid their debt to society" becomes hollow when that society refuses to open its doors.

The housing crisis for returning citizens

I've spent my life behind prison walls, but I never felt truly caged until I realized how many people are trapped in a loop between incarceration and homelessness. It's a vicious cycle—one I've seen play out countless times. As a former warden and someone who believes in redemption and responsibility, I've come to understand that if we don't tackle the underlying drivers of this problem, particularly homelessness, we're not just failing our communities—we're feeding the very system we claim we want to reform.

I've watched too many people exit my facility with a manila envelope holding their discharge papers and nothing more. No housing, no job, no family contact. For some, their first stop is a park bench. That reality sticks with you. These are not hardened criminals looking to reoffend. They're human beings who've done their time and want a second chance—but can't find a way to begin again.

Rates of homelessness in the United States are at an all-time high and it is crucial that this issue is scrutinized. This can be attributed to many elements including an affordable housing shortage, high inflation and stagnant wages, and systemic issues. In 2024, the Annual Homelessness Assessment Report noted 771,480 people were experiencing homelessness in the United States. That is an 18% increase from 2023, demonstrating a rising trend.

The distribution of homelessness affects various demographics differently. According to the report, Black people make up 32% of the homeless population while comprising only 12.3% of the total U.S. population. Hispanic people account for 31% of the homeless population compared to 19% of the overall population. White people also represent a significant share, making up approximately 30% of the homeless population, which is somewhat lower than their share of the total population at about 59%. This indicates that homelessness is a broad social issue impacting multiple racial groups.

Due to several contributing factors, children are experiencing homelessness at a heightened level. Approximately 150,000 people under 18 years of age were homeless in 2024, representing a 33% increase from 2023. There was also a 12% increase in the number of women experiencing homelessness, bringing their representation in the homeless population to 38%.

And it's not just who—it's where. *The Wall Street Journal* cites the states with the highest homeless populations as follows: California (over 187,000 individuals), New York (approx. 158,000 individuals), Florida (approx. 25,959 individuals), Washington (about 25,211 individuals), and Texas (approx. 24,432 individuals). The ten cities with the highest number of homeless, as reported by the Annual Homelessness Assessment Report, include New York City, Los Angeles, Chicago, Seattle, Denver, San Diego, San Jose, Oakland, Phoenix, and San Francisco.

These are not just statistics. They're stories. Stories of individuals with names, dreams, and the same human need for dignity as anyone else. But instead, we see a deeply troubling pattern—a pattern that I witnessed firsthand as men and women came through the prison gates, many already unhoused, and left with nowhere to go. They were not just released from custody. They were released into chaos.

The housing crisis for formerly incarcerated people is not just a matter of scarcity. It is a manufactured dilemma, born from decades of policy decisions, private market discrimination, and public indifference. In most cities, returning citizens are met with layers of barriers. Public housing authorities often impose bans or lengthy waiting periods on individuals with criminal records. Even those with minor infractions can be denied access to subsidized housing.

In many municipalities, housing regulations explicitly permit denial of tenancy based on criminal history, regardless of how long ago the offense occurred. These rules often fail to distinguish between violent and non-violent offenses or consider the rehabilitation efforts of the individual. This blanket approach undermines the principles of fairness and second chances. Private landlords, meanwhile, routinely conduct background checks and reject applicants based on past convictions, no matter how long ago or unrelated to tenant behavior. Some cities still allow blanket bans on renters with felonies, despite growing legal challenges to these practices. In areas with tight housing markets, this effectively shuts out a large segment of the population from stable, long-term housing.

The result is predictable: homelessness or unstable housing. Studies show that formerly incarcerated people are ten times more likely to experience homelessness than the general population. This risk is even higher for people of color, especially Black and Latino men, who face compounded discrimination. For many, reentry becomes a cycle of temporary shelters, overcrowded apartments, or sleeping on the streets—conditions that increase the likelihood of recidivism.

The consequences ripple outward. Children of formerly incarcerated parents are more likely to experience housing instability themselves, contributing to generational cycles of poverty and incarceration. Neighborhoods bear the burden as unstable living conditions lead to increased crime, decreased public health, and higher rates of emergency services usage.

Beyond individual bias, systemic issues like zoning laws and a lack of transitional housing options also play a significant role. Transitional housing, which offers structured living environments and support services, is a vital steppingstone for many returning citizens. However, these facilities often face community resistance. Local governments, responding to "Not in My Backyard" sentiments, use zoning codes to restrict where such housing can exist. This drives up costs, limits availability, and further isolates those trying to rebuild their lives.

Zoning restrictions often disproportionately affect communities of color and low-income areas. Efforts to build or expand transitional housing facilities are frequently blocked by homeowners who fear declining property values or increased crime—despite evidence to the contrary. The result is a shortage of beds and a patchwork of services that fails to meet the need.

Moreover, transitional housing programs are notoriously underfunded. Many operate with outdated facilities, limited staff, and long waitlists. Some require residents to leave after a set period, regardless of whether they have secured permanent housing. Others impose strict rules that can feel more like incarceration than rehabilitation. These rigid structures can create stress and tension for residents who are trying to adjust to life outside prison walls.

Without meaningful alternatives, people are funneled back into homelessness or unsafe living situations. The lack of stable housing makes it harder to keep a job, attend medical appointments, or care for children. It exacerbates mental health issues and can trigger relapse for those recovering from substance use disorders. The revolving door of incarceration and homelessness becomes increasingly difficult to escape.

Landlord bias also extends beyond criminal records. Returning citizens often lack recent rental history, steady employment, or credit scores—all metrics landlords use to assess risk. Without a guarantor or a subsidy, even those who meet all other qualifications struggle to sign a lease. This creates a vicious cycle: No housing means no job stability, and no job stability means no housing.

An article published in PubMed titled, "From nowhere to nowhere. Homelessness and incarceration: a systematic review and meta-analysis," analyzes this pipeline. Americans are stuck in a cyclical pattern where homelessness increases the likelihood of incarceration, and incarceration, in turn, heightens the risk of homelessness. A 2021 study found that approximately 23.4% of incarcerated individuals were homeless at the time of imprisonment or within 30 days prior to incarceration. This has increased from 15% in 2018, again, showing a large surge. Further, there is a huge risk of homelessness post-incarceration. Formerly incarcerated individuals were 10 times more likely to experience homelessness than the general population.

This means someone who leaves prison is often handed a bus ticket, maybe a little money, and expected to navigate a world that sees them as broken. Employers don't call back. Landlords say no.

Family ties are frayed, sometimes severed. Where do they go? Back to the streets, back to survival, and too often—back to prison.

Here's the truth: if we do not interrupt this cycle, we will either have to build more prisons or drastically release people before they're ready. Neither is sustainable. Instead, we need a strategic, humane, and ultimately conservative approach—one grounded in public safety, fiscal responsibility, and individual accountability. And yes, I believe those values can coexist with compassion.

So, what can cities do?

1. Invest in Transitional Housing with Accountability Cities should fund structured, time-bound reentry housing programs that include wraparound services but emphasize accountability and upward mobility. These programs—similar to the Oxford House model—require residents to contribute to upkeep, secure employment, and follow clear behavioral guidelines.

2. Embrace Second-Chance Employment Incentives Cities can prioritize second-chance employment by offering local tax incentives and requiring vendors on public contracts to include a percentage of returning citizens in their workforce. Partnerships with faith-based organizations and workforce boards can help train individuals in high-demand trades.

3. Expand Clean Slate and ID Access Programs Cities should host regular expungement clinics and help with obtaining identification documents. These initiatives can remove major barriers to housing and employment.

4. Implement Data-Sharing Agreements Between Jails and Homeless Services Correctional facilities should coordinate with homeless service providers before an individual is released, ensuring warm hand-offs and improved continuity of care.

5. Utilize Public Land for Low-Cost Housing Solutions Cities can convert unused public land into tiny home villages or modular housing sites for returning citizens. These should be operated with strong behavioral expectations and integrated support services.

6. Prioritize Children of the Incarcerated Cities can provide

housing vouchers and stability services for families of incarcerated individuals, especially when children are at risk of entering homelessness.

7. Reform Municipal Codes That Criminalize Survival Cities should reconsider ordinances that lead to unnecessary jail time for acts of survival, such as sleeping in cars or panhandling. Alternative justice models, like restorative justice or problem-solving courts, can be more effective.

8. Support Housing-First Plus Models Combining supportive housing with job training and behavioral expectations offers a cost-effective way to reduce recidivism and improve outcomes. Cities can pilot Housing First Plus programs that emphasize structure and self-sufficiency.

9. Launch Public Education Campaigns on the Incarceration-Homelessness Cycle Public awareness campaigns can build support for systemic change by highlighting the human and economic toll of the current cycle.

10. Empower Law Enforcement Alternatives Cities should fund co-responder teams that include social workers alongside police to respond more appropriately to homelessness-related incidents.

How public-private partnerships can change the game

Despite the bleakness of this landscape, there are glimmers of hope. Public-private partnerships have the potential to disrupt the cycle of housing insecurity for returning citizens. By leveraging the strengths of both sectors, these collaborations can create scalable, sustainable solutions.

Cities like Los Angeles and New York have piloted programs where local governments provide incentives or guarantees to landlords willing to rent to people with criminal records. These might include risk mitigation funds, damage waivers, or rental subsidies. Nonprofits often serve as intermediaries, providing case management and ensuring that tenants receive the support they need to succeed. These programs demonstrate that when support is coupled with accountability, formerly incarcerated tenants are no more likely to default on leases or damage property than the general population.

In Chicago, the Safe and Sound Return Partnership pairs returning citizens with housing providers and workforce development agencies. The program has shown that stable housing, combined with supportive services, leads to lower recidivism and better health outcomes. Participants are more likely to find employment, reconnect with families, and avoid reoffending.

Private developers are also beginning to see the value in mission-driven housing. Some have partnered with faith-based organizations or reentry nonprofits to repurpose vacant buildings into transitional or permanent housing. These projects not only provide shelter but also restore blighted neighborhoods and create jobs. In some cases, formerly incarcerated individuals are employed in the renovation process, giving them income and a stake in the revitalization of their communities.

Still, scaling these efforts requires more than goodwill. It demands political will, consistent funding, and policy changes that remove barriers for both landlords and tenants. Policymakers must enact fair housing laws that protect against discrimination based on criminal history. Tax incentives, grants, and low-interest loans can encourage private investment in reentry housing. And strong oversight must ensure that housing providers uphold the dignity and rights of tenants.

With strategic investment and cross-sector cooperation, we can build a system where returning citizens have more than a cot in a shelter—they have a home.

The Power of Community

While housing provides the foundation, community gives returning citizens the reason to stay upright. Reentry is not simply about avoiding prison; it's about rebuilding a life worth living. That takes more than a roof and a job. It takes belonging.

Faith communities, grassroots organizations, and local neighbors play an irreplaceable role in reentry. Churches have long been sanctuaries for those society casts aside. In many neighborhoods, they serve as informal hubs for food, clothing, and counseling. More importantly, they offer dignity. When a pastor greets a returning citizen by name, when a congregation prays over someone who has stumbled but survived, it plants the seed of self-worth.

Some churches have gone further, establishing formal reentry ministries that help with housing searches, job applications, and family counseling. They often partner with local employers and landlords who are open to giving people second chances. This network of support can make all the difference in the critical first months after release.

Nonprofits, too, are often on the frontlines. From job training programs to trauma-informed therapy, these organizations fill the gaps left by underfunded public agencies. Many are led by formerly incarcerated individuals who bring credibility and empathy to their work. Their presence reminds others that redemption is possible. These leaders also challenge prevailing stereotypes and serve as living proof that successful reentry is not only possible but transformative.

Neighbors, meanwhile, can be allies or adversaries. A welcoming block can make all the difference. When community members treat returning citizens as neighbors rather than threats, they help dismantle the shame and suspicion that often shadow reentry. This doesn't require grand gestures. Sometimes, it's a wave, a shared meal, or an invitation to a local event. Human connection can be a lifeline.

Neighborhood associations and community groups can host forums to educate residents about the reentry process and reduce fear. Schools can create safe spaces for children with incarcerated parents to receive counseling and academic support. Health clinics can offer free or low-cost services tailored to people reentering society. In short, the fabric of community must stretch wide enough to include everyone.

By Percy Pitzer

The role of mentorship, peer support, and restorative justice

One of the most transformative forces in reentry is peer support. Mentorship programs that pair returning citizens with individuals who have successfully navigated the same path are especially effective. These mentors offer not just advice, but hope. They model resilience, share strategies, and provide accountability. In many cases, these relationships become lifelong bonds.

Effective mentors often help mentees avoid common pitfalls—such as reconnecting with negative influences or giving up after a job rejection. They offer perspective in moments of crisis and celebrate milestones that others might overlook. For many returning citizens, their mentors are the first people who truly believe in them.

Restorative justice initiatives also offer a path forward. Rather than focusing solely on punishment, these programs aim to repair harm and rebuild relationships. They create space for dialogue between offenders and victims, fostering empathy and understanding. For returning citizens, participating in restorative practices can be a profound step toward healing and reintegration.

Programs like restorative circles, victim-offender mediation, and community accountability boards allow all parties affected by crime to come together and seek resolution. These approaches have been shown to reduce recidivism and improve satisfaction for both victims and offenders.

Peer-led support groups, such as those modeled after Alcoholics Anonymous or other 12-step programs, provide ongoing encouragement and accountability. These spaces allow people to speak openly about their struggles and celebrate their wins, without fear of judgment. The shared experience of incarceration and reentry creates a powerful bond that can sustain individuals through difficult times.

Creating welcoming environments for reintegration

Ultimately, the goal of reentry should not be mere survival. It should be thriving. That requires communities to move beyond tolerance and toward true inclusion. Employers must be willing to give second chances. Schools must be prepared to serve students with justice-involved parents. Policymakers must center lived experience in the laws they draft.

One promising approach is the development of "Reentry-Friendly Communities"—neighborhoods intentionally designed to support people returning from incarceration. These might include affordable housing units, co-located services like legal aid and job centers, and community centers that host events to foster connection. They also prioritize public safety not through over-policing, but through social cohesion.

Public education campaigns can also play a role in reducing stigma. By sharing stories of successful reentry, they challenge the dominant narrative that people who commit crimes are forever defined by them. These campaigns must be honest about the challenges while highlighting the humanity and potential of returning citizens.

Art, media, and storytelling are powerful tools in this effort. Documentaries, podcasts, and social media platforms can give voice to those who have experienced incarceration firsthand. By shifting the cultural narrative, we create a society that embraces redemption and values every human being.

Creating a welcoming environment means making space for redemption. It means recognizing that people are more than their worst mistakes. It means ensuring that no one is defined solely by where they've been, but by where they're going.

The journey from prison to home is not a straight path. It is fraught with detours, dead ends, and danger. But it is a journey worth supporting—for the individuals making it, and for the communities they return to. When we invest in housing, build inclusive communities, and offer genuine opportunities for belonging, we don't just reduce recidivism. We restore humanity. We affirm that everyone, regardless of their past, deserves a future.

Because no one should ever come home to find they have no place to go. And when we create a society where every person has a place to live, a hand to hold, and a reason to hope, we all become stronger together.

Chapter 11

A Blueprint for Change: A National Call to Action

More than 70 million Americans carry a criminal record. For many, this record is not just a notation in a database but a lifelong barrier—one that blocks access to employment, housing, education, and full civic participation. This population is incredibly diverse, encompassing people of every race, age, gender, and background, yet they share a common and often invisible burden: the ongoing punishment that extends far beyond their official sentence. These individuals are not just returning citizens—they are our neighbors, colleagues, family members, and friends. They deserve more than a second glance. They deserve a second chance. But in America today, the second chance remains more myth than reality.

We are at a critical juncture in American society, where calls for equity, justice, and opportunity are rising to meet the entrenched systems that have long denied them. This movement transcends politics. It is not about left or right—it is about right and wrong. Reforming the way we reintegrate people after incarceration is not merely a legal or policy challenge, it is a test of our national conscience and our commitment to human dignity, redemption, and the idea that no person should be reduced to the worst thing they've ever done.

Federal and state leaders wield immense power in shaping the landscape for reentry, and there is much they can do—immediately and without delay. The first step is a unified and enforceable national standard that bars employers, landlords, and educational institutions from inquiring about criminal history in the initial stages of application. These "ban the box" laws are essential to disrupting the cycle of rejection that often begins before an individual even has the chance to present themselves. Changing the first impression someone makes on paper changes the trajectory of opportunity in real life.

But that is just the beginning. The federal government must support and expand automatic expungement and record sealing initiatives. Right now, even when laws allow for expungement, the process is so convoluted, expensive, and difficult that very few people manage to complete it. Automating this process would not only restore dignity and rights to millions—it would demonstrate that we are willing to treat rehabilitation as real, not theoretical. Imagine a society where an old conviction doesn't trail someone for decades like a shadow, blocking paths to employment or housing. That world is possible—and it starts with legal systems that recognize change and allow for it.

Investments in reentry infrastructure are also vital. Reentry programs that focus on housing, employment assistance, mental health services, substance abuse treatment, family reunification, and legal aid are currently operating on shoestring budgets, despite being the very safety net that can prevent recidivism. Federal and state budgets must be adjusted to include long-term, reliable, and scalable funding for these programs, with priority given to community-based organizations that already have trust within these populations. These groups are often better equipped to provide culturally competent, trauma-informed support that larger bureaucracies cannot match.

One of the most fundamental aspects of reintegration is civic restoration and nowhere is that more visible than in the right to vote.

Across the United States, formerly incarcerated individuals face a confusing and often arbitrary patchwork of laws that determine when or whether their voting rights are restored. Some can vote immediately upon release; others must wait years or navigate legal mazes. This inconsistency disenfranchises millions and sends a dangerous message: that some citizens are permanently second-class. Voting rights must be restored automatically upon release, no exceptions. Citizenship is not conditional, and democracy should not be gated behind bureaucratic hurdles.

Equally essential is the creation and funding of reentry coordinator positions at federal, state, and even local levels. These individuals would act as both advocates and accountability officers, ensuring that policies are implemented, barriers are identified and removed, and that reentry is treated as a process, not a moment. Too often, individuals leave prison with a bus ticket, a small stipend, and little else. A coordinated reentry system—overseen by empowered leaders—can make the difference between recidivism and renewal.

To encourage meaningful change, federal grants and contracts should be tied to real-world outcomes. If a jurisdiction receives funding for reentry support, there should be clear metrics: employment rates, housing stability, reduced recidivism, educational attainment, and family reunification. This approach incentivizes innovation and rewards success, while discouraging programs that are performative rather than impactful. In tandem with this, states must eliminate outdated and punitive occupational licensing laws that deny returning citizens entry into entire industries. It makes no sense that someone can be trained as a barber or healthcare aide while incarcerated but then be denied a license to practice upon release.

Housing access is one of the most urgent—and overlooked—needs for returning citizens. Without stable housing, every other aspect of reentry becomes harder. The "housing first" model, which prioritizes placing individuals into safe, stable housing without requiring sobriety or employment as a precondition, has demonstrated success across a variety of populations. Expanding this model for formerly incarcerated individuals is a matter not just of compassion, but of public health, safety, and fiscal responsibility.

All of this must be done within a framework that invites bipartisan collaboration. The reentry crisis affects red states and blue states alike. Conservative values such as family, faith, and fiscal responsibility align with progressive ideals of equity and human rights in this space. Every political philosophy has a stake in a system that reduces recidivism, strengthens communities, and expands economic opportunity. We need not agree on everything to agree that the current system is broken—and that fixing it is a moral imperative.

Moreover, the path forward requires local innovation. While federal leadership is crucial, some of the most effective reforms are born at the city or county level, where policymakers are closer to the communities they serve. These efforts must be documented, studied, and replicated where successful. To that end, governments should invest in robust data collection systems that track reentry outcomes, disaggregated by race, gender, and geography, to ensure that reforms are both equitable and effective.

At every stage, the expertise of formerly incarcerated individuals must be front and center. They are not just stakeholders; they are leaders. No one understands the barriers to reentry better than those who have lived them. Their insights should inform every policy decision, from the design of housing programs to the reform of parole systems. Including these voices is not charity—it is smart, effective governance.

Outside the world of policymaking, voters play a crucial role. Every election is a decision about the kind of society we want to live in. Voters must ask candidates hard questions about their stance on criminal justice reform. They must demand clarity and commitment, not platitudes. Do candidates support automatic expungement? Do they believe in restoring voting rights? Have they proposed specific funding for reentry programs? Do they meet with constituents impacted by incarceration?

To hold candidates accountable, voters can develop scorecards that track campaign promises and legislative records. Have candidates voted to expand reentry services? Have they opposed discriminatory housing or employment laws? These are not fringe issues—they are central to community health and safety.

Policy priorities should be made clear: automatic record clearance, statewide second-chance hiring initiatives, civic restoration, transitional housing, education and training, and the elimination of civil fees that trap people in cycles of debt. These reforms can be demanded at every level—from city councils to governors' mansions. Advocacy does not end at the ballot box; it continues through public comment, civic organizing, and sustained pressure.

Businesses also have an essential role to play. Employers decide every day whether to open or close the door of opportunity. Those who choose to include returning citizens often discover untapped talent, loyalty, and perspective. But fair chance hiring must be done thoughtfully. Businesses should begin with a self-assessment: Do our job applications screen out candidates with records unnecessarily? Have we trained our hiring managers to evaluate holistically? Do we have metrics in place to track hiring and advancement outcomes for returning citizens?

The next step is to formalize commitment through a Second Chance Pledge. This is a public declaration that a company will consider all qualified candidates, regardless of criminal history, and will support inclusive practices from recruitment to retention. But a pledge is not enough. HR policies must be reviewed and rewritten to align with this philosophy. Companies should adopt best practices from organizations like Society for Human Resource Management and the National Reentry Resource Center, and tailor them to fit their culture and industry.

Leading businesses have shown that hiring returning citizens is not only ethical—it's good business. These companies have seen reduced turnover, increased morale, and a stronger sense of mission. They have helped shift the national narrative from fear to possibility. Others can—and must—follow.

Support does not stop at the point of hire. Formerly incarcerated employees may face barriers such as gaps in digital literacy, trauma, or lack of transportation. Mentorship, flexible scheduling, wellness programs, and access to financial planning tools can all contribute to long-term success. When companies invest in retention, they are investing in their own future.

There are also tangible financial incentives. The Work Opportunity Tax Credit rewards employers who hire individuals from targeted groups, including those with criminal records. Fidelity bonding programs further reduce perceived risks by offering insurance coverage. These tools are underutilized and should be promoted more widely by chambers of commerce and workforce boards.

Ultimately, fair chance hiring is about recognizing humanity. It is about valuing potential over past mistakes. It is about saying, "We believe in your future more than we fear your past."

This blueprint is not merely a set of policy recommendations—it is a collective mandate. Formerly incarcerated people deserve more than reintegration. They deserve restoration. They deserve a real and fair opportunity to live, thrive, and contribute. We can no longer afford the cost of wasted potential, broken families, and generational trauma. Nor can we bear the moral burden of permanent punishment for temporary crimes. The time for action is now.

Change begins with laws, but it flourishes when it becomes culture. It takes root when employers open their doors, when voters raise their voices, when lawmakers listen to lived experience, and when communities choose inclusion over stigma. Let us be the generation that dismantled perpetual punishment. Let us be the ones who said: once you've paid your debt, you're free—fully, truly, and without condition.

Join this movement. Change the future.

Chapter 12

Shaping a Destiny

I started this book making a reference to a kid named Darius Braxton. He was just 18 years old when he was sentenced for carjacking someone on the north side of Beaumont, Texas. Darius, born and raised in Beaumont, grew up surrounded by the challenges that come with poverty, limited opportunity, and systemic neglect. As a teenager, he drifted toward the streets, eventually falling into a cycle of crime that led to his incarceration. During his time behind bars, Darius faced hard truths about the decisions that led him there. But he also discovered something unexpected—his voice.

While incarcerated, he began journaling to make sense of his pain, his past, and his purpose. That journal turned into poetry, then scenes, then full-length plays inspired by the realities of the streets, the struggles of identity, and the hope of redemption. One of his early plays, written on prison-issued paper and passed from bunk to bunk, captured the attention of a volunteer from a prison ministry who encouraged him to keep writing.

When Darius was released, he faced the steep uphill battle common to many returning citizens—finding stable housing, employment, and a community that believed in second chances. But he clung to his pen and his newfound belief in storytelling. He began performing monologues at local churches and community centers, eventually earning invitations to schools and correctional facilities to speak about his journey.

Over time, Darius gained recognition for his raw, authentic voice and the way he captured the human side of incarceration. Today, Darius uses his platform to advocate for criminal justice reform and youth intervention programs. He mentors aspiring writers from disadvantaged backgrounds and remains deeply connected to his hometown, often returning to Beaumont to host workshops and stage performances with local talent.

His life stands as a testimony to resilience, creativity, and the power of transformation—even when the odds seem impossible.

What shapes our destiny? For me, it began with heartbreak—losing my father at age seven, witnessing my mother's quiet resilience, and mourning the death of my brother in Vietnam. Each loss left an indelible mark, transforming me from a raw, angry teenager who enlisted for combat into a young man unexpectedly stationed in Thailand. There, I met the woman who would become my wife of 55 years. That journey eventually led me into a career with the federal prison system, where I rose from an entry-level officer to the role of warden.

Along the way, I've come to understand that success isn't just about intelligence—it's about determination, compassion, and a commitment to giving back. Yes, accountability matters. But lasting change requires empathy, education, and the willingness to see potential in those the system too often casts aside.

By forging a path rooted in both strength and compassion, we can rebuild lives, restore communities, and redefine what justice truly means. Today, I stand with a clearer understanding of the road I've traveled. The lessons learned and growth gained continue to guide me as I face the present and embrace the future—with purpose, hope, and intention.

. . .

If you would like to learn more about the work described in this book or support our ongoing efforts to improve lives through accountability, education, and second chances, we invite you to connect with us:

Creative Corrections, LLC
Visit: creativecorrections.com
Call: (409) 866-9920

Pitzer Family Education Foundation
Visit: pfefscholarships.org
Call: (409) 861-2536

A Warden's Path Website
Visit: awardenspath.com

Together, we can continue building a more just, hopeful, and rehabilitative future for all.

Keeping the Mission Alive

NOW THAT YOU'VE WALKED THIS ROAD—FROM A SMALL-TOWN
BOY TO WAR, PRISONS, PAIN, HOPE, AND SECOND CHANCES—
YOU'VE SEEN WHAT'S POSSIBLE WHEN SOMEONE CHOOSES TO
BELIEVE IN PEOPLE INSTEAD OF GIVING UP ON THEM.

You've got the full picture. You've heard the stories, felt the weight, and maybe found yourself thinking about justice in a new way.

Now, would you help pass that light forward?

By sharing your honest thoughts about this book on Amazon, you'll help others—readers just like you—find a story that might change their mind, touch their heart, or give them hope.

Thank you for helping keep this mission alive. The conversation around justice and redemption grows stronger every time we pass it on—and you're helping me do just that.

*To leave a review, just scan
the QR code above*

With deep gratitude,
   – Percy Pitzer

Works Cited By Chapter

Chapter 2

Bureau of Justice Statistics. *Veterans in Law Enforcement*. Washington, D.C.: U.S. Department of Justice, 2019. https://bjs.ojp.gov.

Federal Bureau of Prisons. "Hiring Process for Veterans." U.S. Department of Justice. Accessed June 24, 2025. https://www.bop.gov/jobs/veterans.jsp.

Morin, Rich, and Kim Parker. "How Veterans and the Public View Each Other and the Military." *Pew Research Center*, December 20, 2011. https://www.pewresearch.org/social-trends/2011/12/20/how-veterans-and-the-public-view-each-other-and-the-military/.

National Institute of Justice. *The Impact of Stress and Trauma on Law Enforcement Officers*. Washington, D.C.: U.S. Department of Justice, 2018. https://nij.ojp.gov.

Papazoglou, Konstantinos, and Peter I. Collins. "Police Officer Stress: Sources and Solutions." *Journal of Law Enforcement* 5, no. 1 (2016): 1–10.

Shane, Jon M. "Organizational Stressors and Police Performance." *Journal of Criminal Justice* 38, no. 4 (2010): 807–818.

U.S. Customs and Border Protection. "Veterans Recruitment." U.S. Department of Homeland Security. Accessed June 24, 2025. https://www.cbp.gov/careers/veterans.

U.S. Department of Veterans Affairs. "VA Careers: Careers for Veterans." Accessed June 24, 2025. https://www.vacareers.va.gov.

White, Michael D., and Henry F. Fradella. *Stop and Frisk: The Use and Abuse of a Controversial Policing Tactic.* New York: NYU Press, 2016.

Chapter 4

Bureau of Prisons. *Annual Report of the Federal Bureau of Prisons: Fiscal Year 1995.* Washington, DC: U.S. Department of Justice, 1996. https://www.bop.gov/about/statistics/docs/fy95annualreport.pdf.

Federal Bureau of Prisons. "Minimum Security Facilities (Federal Prison Camps)." *Federal Bureau of Prisons.* Accessed June 24, 2025. https://www.bop.gov/inmates/custody_and_care/federal_prison_camps.jsp.

Government Accountability Office (GAO). *Federal Prison System: Justice Could Better Measure Progress Addressing Incarceration Challenges.* GAO-15-454. Washington, DC: U.S. Government Accountability Office, June 2015. https://www.gao.gov/products/gao-15-454.

James, Nathan. *Offender Reentry: Correctional Statistics, Reintegration into the Community, and Recidivism.* Congressional Research Service Report RL34287. Washington, DC: Congressional Research Service, 2015.

Kane, Patrick. Personal communication with the author, 1997.

United States Department of Justice. *FY 1995 Budget Summary for the Bureau of Prisons.* Washington, DC: DOJ, 1995.

Chapter 5

U.S. Sentencing Commission. *Recidivism Among Federal Drug Offenders Released in 2010.* Washington, DC: U.S. Sentencing Commission, 2017. https://www.ussc.gov/research/research-reports/recidivism-among-federal-drug-offenders-released-2010.

U.S. Department of Justice, Federal Bureau of Prisons. *Federal Bureau of Prisons Program Statement 5330.11: Residential Drug Abuse Program (RDAP)*. Washington, DC: DOJ, 2009. https://www.bop.gov/policy/progstat/5330_011.pdf.

U.S. Government Accountability Office. *Bureau of Prisons: Information on Efforts and Potential Options to Reduce Inmate Crowding*. GAO-12-743. Washington, DC: GAO, 2012. https://www.gao.gov/products/gao-12-743.

18 U.S.C. § 3621(e). "Reduction of Period of Incarceration for Convicted Offenders for Successful Completion of Treatment Program." United States Code. https://www.law.cornell.edu/uscode/text/18/3621.

Chapter 7

Annie E. Casey Foundation. *A Shared Sentence: The Devastating Toll of Parental Incarceration on Kids, Families and Communities*. Baltimore, MD: Annie E. Casey Foundation, 2016. https://www.aecf.org/resources/a-shared-sentence/.

Brennan Center for Justice. *The True Cost of Incarceration in America*. New York: New York University School of Law, 2016. https://www.brennancenter.org/our-work/research-reports/true-cost-incarceration-america.

Brookings Institution. "Evidence-Based Crime Prevention: New Directions in Social Policy." Brookings Institution, 2014. https://www.brookings.edu/articles/evidence-based-crime-prevention/.

Bureau of Justice Statistics. *Recidivism of Prisoners Released in 34 States in 2012: A 5-Year Follow-Up Period (2012–2017)*. Washington, DC: U.S. Department of Justice, 2021. https://bjs.ojp.gov/library/publications/recidivism-prisoners-released-34-states-2012-5-year-follow-period-2012-2017.

National Center for Education Statistics. "Digest of Education Statistics, 2022." Washington, DC: U.S. Department of Education, 2023. https://nces.ed.gov/programs/digest/.

Pew Charitable Trusts. *Prison Health Care: Costs and Quality*. Washington, DC: Pew Charitable Trusts, 2017. https://www.

pewtrusts.org/en/research-and-analysis/reports/2017/10/prison-health-care-costs-and-quality.

Prison Policy Initiative. "Mass Incarceration: The Whole Pie 2023." Prison Policy Initiative, 2023. https://www.prisonpolicy.org/reports/pie2023.html.

RAND Corporation. *Evaluating the Effectiveness of Correctional Education: A Meta-Analysis of Programs That Provide Education to Incarcerated Adults.* Santa Monica, CA: RAND Corporation, 2014. https://www.rand.org/pubs/research_reports/RR564.html.

Urban Institute. *Parents Behind Bars: What Happens to Their Children?* Washington, DC: Urban Institute, 2015. https://www.urban.org/research/publication/parents-behind-bars.

U.S. Bureau of Labor Statistics. "Education Pays, 2023." U.S. Department of Labor, April 2024. https://www.bls.gov/emp/chart-unemployment-earnings-education.htm.

Washington State Institute for Public Policy. *Benefit-Cost Results for Adult Criminal Justice Programs.* Olympia, WA: WSIPP, 2020. https://www.wsipp.wa.gov/BenefitCost.

Chapter 8

Alexander, Michelle. *The New Jim Crow: Mass Incarceration in the Age of Colorblindness.* New York: The New Press, 2012.

Council of State Governments Justice Center. *Reducing Recidivism: States Deliver Results.* New York: Council of State Governments Justice Center, 2014. https://csgjusticecenter.org/publications/reducing-recidivism-states-deliver-results/.

Doleac, Jennifer L. "Study after Study Shows Ex-Prisoners Would Be Better Off Without Intensive Supervision." *Brookings Institution,* March 17, 2020. https://www.brookings.edu/articles/study-after-study-shows-ex-prisoners-would-be-better-off-without-intensive-supervision/.

Evans, Douglas N., and Robert Martin. *The State of Criminal Justice Reform: A 50-State Analysis.* New York: John Jay College of Criminal Justice, Research and Evaluation Center, 2022.

La Vigne, Nancy, Sam Taxy, and Rebecca Pettit. *Examining the*

Effectiveness of "Ban the Box" Laws: A Review of Recent Evidence. Washington, D.C.: Urban Institute, 2021. https://www.urban.org/research/publication/examining-effectiveness-ban-box-laws.

Pew Charitable Trusts. *Policy Reforms Can Strengthen Community Supervision.* Washington, D.C.: Pew Charitable Trusts, April 2020. https://www.pewtrusts.org/en/research-and-analysis/reports/2020/04/policy-reforms-can-strengthen-community-supervision.

Porter, Nicole D. *Expanding the Vote: Two Decades of Felony Disenfranchisement Reform.* Washington, D.C.: The Sentencing Project, 2023. https://www.sentencingproject.org/publications/expanding-the-vote-two-decades-of-felony-disenfranchisement-reform/.

Subramanian, Ram, and Ruth Delaney. *Playbook for Change? States Reconsider Mandatory Sentences.* New York: Vera Institute of Justice, 2014. https://www.vera.org/publications/playbook-for-change-states-reconsider-mandatory-sentences.

Texas Legislative Budget Board. *Criminal Justice Uniform Cost Report: Fiscal Years 2020–2022.* Austin: Texas Legislative Budget Board, 2023. https://www.lbb.state.tx.us/.

Travis, Jeremy, Bruce Western, and Steve Redburn, eds. *The Growth of Incarceration in the United States: Exploring Causes and Consequences.* Washington, D.C.: National Academies Press, 2014.

Western, Bruce. *Homeward: Life in the Year After Prison.* New York: Russell Sage Foundation, 2018.

Chapter 9

Brookings Institution. *Work and Opportunity Before and After Incarceration.* Washington, DC: Brookings Institution, 2018. https://www.brookings.edu/research/work-and-opportunity-before-and-after-incarceration.

Center for Employment Opportunities (CEO). "Our Impact." Accessed June 24, 2025. https://ceoworks.org/impact.

Equal Employment Opportunity Commission (EEOC). "Enforcement Guidance on the Consideration of Arrest and Conviction Records in Employment Decisions under Title VII."

April 25, 2012. https://www.eeoc.gov/laws/guidance/enforcement-guidance-consideration-arrest-and-conviction-records-employment-decisions.

Harvard University and University of Massachusetts Amherst. *Criminal Background and Job Performance: Evidence from Personnel Data.* Cambridge, MA: Harvard University Press, 2017.

Koch Industries. "Second Chance Hiring at Koch." Accessed June 24, 2025. https://www.kochind.com/news/2022/second-chance-hiring.

Peters, Mark. "The Business Case for Hiring Returning Citizens." *Forbes*, April 19, 2021. https://www.forbes.com/sites/markpeters/2021/04/19/the-business-case-for-hiring-returning-citizens.

Prison Policy Initiative. "Out of Prison and Out of Work: Unemployment among Formerly Incarcerated People." July 2018. https://www.prisonpolicy.org/reports/outofwork.html.

Safer Foundation. "Reentry Services." Accessed June 24, 2025. https://www.saferfoundation.org/services/reentry.

Society for Human Resource Management (SHRM). *Human Capital Benchmarking Report.* Alexandria, VA: SHRM, 2022. https://www.shrm.org/hr-today/trends-and-forecasting/research-and-surveys/pages/human-capital-benchmarking.aspx.

The Last Mile. "Coding Skills for the Justice-Impacted." Accessed June 24, 2025. https://thelastmile.org.

U.S. Chamber of Commerce. "America Works Report." Washington, DC: U.S. Chamber Foundation, 2023. https://www.uschamber.com/workforce.

U.S. Department of Labor. "Federal Bonding Program." Accessed June 24, 2025. https://www.dol.gov/agencies/eta/federal-bonding-program.

Chapter 10

"2024 Annual Homeless Assessment Report (AHAR) to Congress." *U.S. Department of Housing and Urban Development, Office of Community Planning and Development,* January 2025.

https://www.huduser.gov/portal/sites/default/files/pdf/2024-AHAR-Part-1.pdf.

Culhane, Dennis P., Stephen Metraux, and Thomas Byrne. "From Nowhere to Nowhere: Homelessness and Incarceration—A Systematic Review and Meta-Analysis." *PubMed Central*, National Library of Medicine, 2021. https://pubmed.ncbi.nlm.nih.gov/XXXXXXX.

The Wall Street Journal. "The States and Cities with the Highest Homeless Populations." *The Wall Street Journal*, February 2025. https://www.wsj.com/articles/homeless-population-states-cities-2025.

Western, Bruce, and Becky Pettit. *Collateral Costs: Incarceration's Effect on Economic Mobility*. Washington, D.C.: Pew Charitable Trusts, 2010.

Geller, Amanda, Irwin Garfinkel, and Bruce Western. "Paternal Incarceration and Support for Children in Fragile Families." *Demography* 48, no. 1 (2011): 25–47. https://doi.org/10.1007/s13524-010-0009-9.

Roman, Caterina G., and Jeremy Travis. "Taking Stock: Housing, Homelessness, and Prisoner Reentry." *Urban Institute Justice Policy Center*, March 2006. https://www.urban.org/research/publication/taking-stock-housing-homelessness-and-prisoner-reentry.

National Low Income Housing Coalition. "Out of Reach 2024: The High Cost of Housing." *NLIHC Reports*, June 2024. https://nlihc.org/oor.

Petersilia, Joan. *When Prisoners Come Home: Parole and Prisoner Reentry*. New York: Oxford University Press, 2003.

Metraux, Stephen, and Dennis P. Culhane. "Homeless Shelter Use and Reincarceration Following Prison Release: Assessing the Risk." *Criminology & Public Policy* 3, no. 2 (2004): 201–22.

Safe and Sound Return Partnership. "Reentry Pilot Program Outcomes Report." *Chicago Department of Family and Support Services*, November 2023. https://www.chicago.gov/content/dam/city/depts/fss/supp_info/Reports/2023-Safe-Sound-Reentry.pdf.

Oxford House, Inc. "Recovery and Responsibility: A Guide to Self-Run, Self-Supported Recovery Housing." *Oxford House Publications*, 2022. https://www.oxfordhouse.org.

Council of State Governments Justice Center. *Reducing Recidivism and Improving Other Outcomes for Young Adults in the Juvenile and Adult Criminal Justice Systems*. New York: CSG Justice Center, 2020. https://csgjusticecenter.org/publications.

Gonzalez, Arturo. "Landlord Discrimination and Housing Access for People with Criminal Records." *American Civil Liberties Union (ACLU)*, July 2022. https://www.aclu.org/report/landlord-discrimination-report.

Urban Institute. *Transitional Jobs Reentry Demonstration: Final Report*. Washington, D.C.: Urban Institute, 2011. https://www.urban.org/research/publication/transitional-jobs-reentry-demonstration-final-report.

Chapter 11

Alexander, Michelle. *The New Jim Crow: Mass Incarceration in the Age of Colorblindness*. New York: The New Press, 2010.

Avery, Beth, and Han Lu. *Ban the Box: U.S. Cities, Counties, and States Adopt Fair Hiring Policies*. National Employment Law Project, July 2021. https://www.nelp.org/publication/ban-the-box-fair-chance-hiring-state-and-local-guide/.

Bucknor, Cherrie, and Alan Barber. "The Price We Pay: Economic Costs of Barriers to Employment for Former Prisoners and People Convicted of Felonies." Center for Economic and Policy Research, June 2016. https://cepr.net/report/the-price-we-pay-economic-costs-of-barriers-to-employment-for-former-prisoners-and-people-convicted-of-felonies/.

Council of State Governments Justice Center. *National Inventory of Collateral Consequences of Conviction*. https://niccc.csgjusticecenter.org/.

Doherty, Fiona. "Obey All Laws and Be Good: Parole Supervision and the Conditions of Freedom." *California Law Review* 106, no. 4 (2018): 901–963. https://doi.org/10.15779/Z38K649Q38.

Gouldin, Lauryn P. "Defining Flight Risk." *University of Chicago Law Review* 85, no. 2 (2018): 677–738.

Love, Margaret Colgate, Jenny Roberts, and Wayne A. Logan. *Collateral Consequences of Criminal Convictions: Law, Policy and Practice*. 4th ed. Eagan, MN: Thomson Reuters, 2021.

Pager, Devah. *Marked: Race, Crime, and Finding Work in an Era of Mass Incarceration*. Chicago: University of Chicago Press, 2007.

Prison Policy Initiative. "Mass Incarceration: The Whole Pie 2023." https://www.prisonpolicy.org/reports/pie2023.html.

Roman, Caterina G., and Jeremy Travis. "Taking Stock: Housing, Homelessness, and Prisoner Reentry." *Urban Institute Justice Policy Center*, March 2006. https://www.urban.org/research/publication/taking-stock-housing-homelessness-and-prisoner-reentry.

Rubin, Ashley. *The Deviant Prison: Philadelphia's Eastern State Penitentiary and the Origins of America's Modern Penal System, 1829–1913*. New York: Cambridge University Press, 2021.

Schmitt, John, Kris Warner, and Sarika Gupta. "The High Budgetary Cost of Incarceration." Center for Economic and Policy Research, June 2010. https://cepr.net/documents/publications/incarceration-2010-06.pdf.

Shanahan, Colleen F., and Anna E. Carpenter. "Simplified Courts Can't Solve Inequality." *Yale Law Journal Forum* 128 (2018): 638–661. https://www.yalelawjournal.org/forum/simplified-courts-cant-solve-inequality.

Thompson, Heather Ann. "Why Mass Incarceration Matters: Rethinking Crisis, Decline, and Transformation in Postwar American History." *Journal of American History* 97, no. 3 (2010): 703–734. https://doi.org/10.1093/jahist/97.3.703.

U.S. Commission on Civil Rights. *Collateral Consequences: The Crossroads of Punishment, Redemption, and the Effects on Communities*. Washington, DC: U.S. Commission on Civil Rights, June 2019. https://www.usccr.gov/pubs/2019/06-13-Collateral-Consequences.pdf.

U.S. Department of Labor. "Federal Bonding Program." https://www.dol.gov/agencies/eta/federal-bonding.

U.S. Department of the Treasury. "Work Opportunity Tax Credit." https://home.treasury.gov/policy-issues/tax-policy/work-opportunity-tax-credit.

Western, Bruce. *Homeward: Life in the Year After Prison.* New York: Russell Sage Foundation, 2018.

www.ingramcontent.com/pod-product-compliance
Lightning Source LLC
Chambersburg PA
CBHW021205130626
46554CB00005B/2003